A Transdisciplinary Study of Addiction

Using novel, bioethical framing alongside critical and comprehensive analysis of harm reduction approaches, this cutting-edge book addresses the multifaceted and transdisciplinary issue of drug addiction in society, exploring how addiction can be conceptualized from various disciplinary perspectives for positive policy outcomes.

The book discusses the philosophical concepts of agency and action within addiction, and how this can support the foundations needed to identify the most effective and ethical harm reduction strategies within policy frameworks. Foregrounding the implications for this notion of agency, chapters trace the evolution of the concept of addiction through the centuries and examine contemporary understandings from neuroscience, philosophy, bioethics, and policy analysis. Comparative, case study analysis is conducted to contrast local, empirically based models for drug policy in the United Kingdom alongside external models based on international treaties, which dictate a top-down approach to drug penalization.

Offering a research-based and theoretically informed framework for effective harm reduction strategies and policies, this book will be of interest to scholars, researchers, and postgraduate students in the fields of addiction studies, bioethics, and mental health policy more broadly. Policymakers working in addictions and substance use may also find the book relevant.

Francisco Blancarte Jaber is a recent doctoral graduate in Law at the University of Edinburgh, UK, and was newly appointed as Head of the Department for Content Creation at the National Bioethics Commission in Mexico.

Explorations in Mental Health

Challenging the Therapeutic Narrative
Historical and Clinical Perspectives on the Genetics of Behavior
Robert G. Goldstein

Critical Resilience and Thriving in Response to Systemic Oppression
Insights to Inform Social Justice in Critical Times
Melissa L. Morgan

Understanding Contemporary Diet Culture through the Lens of Lacanian Psychoanalytic Theor
Eating the Lack
Bethany Morris

Learning the Hard Way in Clinical Internships in Social Work and Psychology
Lessons for Safety, Boundary-Setting, and Deepening the Practicum Experience
Susan A. Lord

Mental Healthcare in Brazilian Spiritism: The Aesthetics of Healing
Helmar Kurz

Exploring Creative Wellbeing Frameworks in Context
Nature, Culture, and Sustainable Futures
Edited by Wenche Torrissen and Helga S. Løvoll

A Transdisciplinary Study of Addiction
A New Framework for Drug Policy Reform
Francisco Blancarte Jaber

For more information about this series, please visit www.routledge.com/Explorations-in-Mental-Health/book-series/EXMH

A Transdisciplinary Study of Addiction

A New Framework for Drug Policy Reform

Francisco Blancarte Jaber

Routledge
Taylor & Francis Group
LONDON AND NEW YORK

First published 2025
by Routledge
4 Park Square, Milton Park, Abingdon, Oxon OX14 4RN

and by Routledge
605 Third Avenue, New York, NY 10158

Routledge is an imprint of the Taylor & Francis Group, an informa business

British Library Cataloguing-in-Publication Data
A catalogue record for this book is available from the British Library

ISBN: 978-1-032-95024-2 (hbk)
ISBN: 978-1-032-95026-6 (pbk)
ISBN: 978-1-003-58290-8 (ebk)

DOI: 10.4324/9781003582908

Typeset in Sabon
by SPi Technologies India Pvt Ltd (Straive)

To Mom and Dad

Contents

Acknowledgements

First and foremost, I would like to dedicate this book to my parents, who have supported me throughout my life and helped me reach this milestone. To my mother, for teaching me the value of responsibility and steadfast dedication to my work. To my father, for teaching me the value of wisdom and the pursuit of academic inquiry in my life.

I would also like to thank both of my academic supervisors, Dr. Agomoni Ganguli-Mitra and Dr. Sarah Chan, for their guidance and invaluable help in shaping the thesis upon which this book is based. I relied heavily on their advice and would not have been able to construct a cohesive work without their constant support.

The process of writing this work was long and at times isolating. It would have been considerably more difficult without the emotional support of my sisters, Paula and Emilia, throughout all these years. My conversations with them have always helped me more than they may realize.

Finally, though I am proud of having completed this task, I am immensely prouder of having completed it in balance with my personal life. That balance, and the reason I was able to maintain happiness and serenity throughout, was entirely due to the love and support of my partner, Ana Victoria.

Introduction

Addiction, not only as a phenomenon but as a concept, is so prevalent in our society that it can be somewhat difficult to parse through what it means, how it works, and why it's a problem that needs solving. There's no confusion about its negative connotation. Even a cheeky admission of guilty pleasure, be it chocolate cake or the latest series on a streaming platform, carries with it the implicit: "I know this is probably not the healthiest choice for me, but I just can't help myself". Most people indeed make a conceptual association between "being addicted to…" and "having a problem with…". But why that connotation?

The word itself, addiction, comes from the Latin root, *dicere*, meaning "to say" or "to speak", as can be seen in the words dictate, diction, and dictionary. *Addicere*, therefore, is a Latin compound of *dicere* and the proposition *ad*, from which the word addiction is directly derived, meaning literally "to speak to" or, more abstractly, "to adjudicate". According to a study published in the journal "Addiction Research and Theory" (Rosenthal & Faris, 2019), *addictio*, the abstract noun derived from the verb, was the Latin technical term for the judicial act by which a debtor became the slave of his creditor. The sentence was pronounced (or dictated) by the judge (praetor), according to the ancient laws of "The Twelve Tables" in the early Roman Republic (5th–3rd century BC).

In that study, the authors explain how "The Twelve Tables" recognized a limited number of solutions for enforcing property rights or contractual claims. On days when the Roman religious calendar permitted judicial proceedings, the *praetor urbanus*, the official in charge, ritually intoned a formula that summarized his judicial powers: *do, dico, addico*, which can be translated as "I give, I say, I adjudge". This pronouncement was a binding ruling, in the sense that in the exercise of his judicial duties, the praetor acted in a quasi-religious capacity. This left the *addictus*, the guilty individual in question, physically chained and delivered to his creditor by the praetor's authority, to be held for 60 days or until the debt was paid. Failure to pay the debt after the statutory 60 days had elapsed made the debtor the permanent

DOI: 10.4324/9781003582908-1

property of his creditor. He could then, at the creditor's discretion, be held, killed, or sold into slavery. Rosenthal and Faris thus provide us with the etymological roots of "being addicted to..." being the underlying concept of "being a slave to...".

We can then understand where this idea comes from: that suffering from an addiction means that our freedom – perhaps in a certain sense our free will – is limited, if not completely annulled. And although the etymological origins of the term are ancient, the most recent advances in the area of neuroscience support this same idea that our capacity to control our decisions and actions, our faculty of self-control, is observably compromised by the use (and especially the abuse) of certain psychoactive substances.

There is indeed a consensus within the neuroscientific literature that addiction can best be understood as a chronic disease of the brain (Leshner, 1997), a consequence of prolonged drug use that results in the loss of control that characterizes the habitual consumption of most addicted people. This area of neuroscience research attempts to uncover the root of the self-control problem frequently associated with addictive behaviour. That is, it attempts to explain why individuals suffering from an addiction disorder behave as if they were "enslaved to the substance they are consuming".

It should be noted that there is a perspective that criticizes this paradigm of "addiction as a brain disease" as a neuroreductionist. Because of this, some attempts have been made to include a social context, a genetic component, and comorbidity with other mental and behavioural disorders in the conceptualization of the paradigm. All of this is with the perspective of understanding addiction within a more "biopsychosocial" framework (Buchman et al., 2010).

Indeed, if the problematization of addiction were limited to the individual sphere, we would not be speaking of a social problem, let alone one of the great archetypal social problems of our time: transversal, globalized, and apparently intractable. Its complexity is daunting and requires a commitment to solving several national and international problems, from socioeconomic inequality and crime, to international development and terrorism. Political leaders line up to talk about the drug problem against which "society must be defended", from the United Nations and the European Union, to a series of national presidents and prime ministers.

For while the consumption of drugs may be ancient (Guerra-Doce, 2015), the notion that certain types of substances, or rather certain types of consumers of such substances, are a problem for society dates back to the beginning of the industrial age and its effect on the conception of the citizen within the Liberal State (Seddon, 2010). This problematization of the consumption of psychoactive substances arose from having to reconcile a need for sobriety in the new mechanical practices that represented most occupations of the workforce, at the advent of the Industrial Revolution, with the economic need for these substances to be widely consumed as part of the trade in goods on which most of the economies of the colonial empires were built (alcohol, tobacco, tea, opium, chocolate, and sugar) (Room, 2006).

Put another way, addiction is a problem because we have made it a problem. The use of psychoactive substances has existed since the beginning of human civilization (perhaps even before), but such use at the societal level does not become a problem until our industrial needs demand that a workforce remain sober, or until certain populations become problematic for political purposes.

Therefore, there should not be a dichotomy between a neurobiological conceptualization of addiction as dependence or a perspective that sees it solely as an irrational behavioural disorder. Addiction is a social construct and therefore, if it is a problem, the solution must also be found through that perspective: social constructivism. We must rethink what we understand by "being addicted to..." or "having a problem with...", in order to put an end to the sociopolitical problem of drugs and propose meaningful solutions to the bioethical problem of addiction.

This book aims to do just that: propose a new way of thinking about addiction, and in doing so, a new way of dealing with people who are addicted. In view of that, this book will attempt to answer the following question:

> How ought addiction be conceptualized in order to construct policy frameworks that treat addicted persons ethically whilst effectively reducing drug-related harms?

To answer this question, my methodology will be to break down this book into distinct sections. I will present two conceptualizations of addiction that have thus far informed policy frameworks. Firstly, I will assess the conceptualization of addiction as a choice dependent upon a rational agent, through the lens of action theory in 20th-century philosophy of action. Secondly, I will review the modelization of addiction as a brain disease through the lens of neuroscientific research on addiction. I will then review the history of drug policy through the lens of a series of milestone legislative events in the United Kingdom. And finally, I will present an argument for harm reduction strategies as a type of policy framework that can address the need for effective reduction of drug-related harms in society with the ethical treatment of addicted persons.

Why is Addiction a Problem?

Addiction is a multifaceted phenomenon. This may appear *prima facie* on certain accounts of addiction as an intractable problem that must be resolved necessarily through the implementation of interdisciplinary dialogue between clinicians, psychologists, social workers, policymakers, and economists.

But although this multifaceted aspect may give the impression that the "problem" of addiction is too unwieldy, we can begin any attempt to resolve the problem of addiction by asking why it is a problem in the first place. What is the origin of the problematization of addiction?

As previously mentioned, the term "addiction" is in itself already loaded, meaning etymologically "to be enslaved to" (Rosenthal & Faris, 2019), i.e. to be tied to something and thus inexorably linked to it. But what is addiction, beyond the linguistic origin of the term? To what does that term refer to ontologically? Is it a physical dependence? Is it a moral condition, the inability to refrain from something? Is it an emergent property resulting from something happening in our brain circuitry? And most importantly, what aspect of it is problematic?

Though the practice of consumption of drugs can be traced back to the earliest records of human civilization (Guerra-Doce, 2015), and we can reasonably infer that such consumption may have led to persons being "addicted" to various substances throughout history, "addiction" as a concept has much more recent beginnings. Harry Levine, in his paper "The Discovery of Addiction", proposed a Foucauldian analysis be applied to the consumption of alcohol and its emergence as a problematic practice in a specific historical context, namely in the early 19th-century United States and the later Victorian era in the United Kingdom. Levine accentuates the Foucauldian power relationships that established themselves between the people consuming alcohol in excessive quantities and the people developing norms and mores in reaction to said excessive consumption. These dynamics were expressed through things like the "temperance" movement that started in New York and Massachusetts at the beginning of the 19th century, and which was later exported towards Ireland and Great Britain, and carried with it a new understanding of drinking and alcoholism as a problem of self-control and moderation (Levine, 1978). Here the concept of addiction emerged as social conditions manifested the need for a conceptualization of a problem brought about by changing mores, and in the view of Levine and contemporary historians, the emergence of addiction is a phenomenon of the late modern period, not entirely dissociated from the new urban structurization of the post-industrial revolution and its consequent effect on work/life routines.

This notion of addiction as a concept that is historically and culturally specific falls in line with the perspective that classifies not only drinking but substance abuse in general, as culturally specific. Robin Room argues, for example, that addiction is so culturally specific that it merits the label of a "culture-bound syndrome" (Room, 1985), a condition inherently tied to the way of thinking in European cultures. This conceptualization proposes that sociocultural factors influence drug consumption in several ways, both predicting and correlating with the "problematic" consumption of the substance in question. The locus of the disease, if indeed it is thought of as one, is expanded outside of the individual's physical body to inhabit the "*supraindividual*", sociocultural level (Room, 1985). The idea of the physical dependence upon the substance, one of the many clinical conceptualizations of addiction, is then bound to a specific cultural context that is dependent on social and cultural characteristics of a particular time and place, for it to be of any meaning and useful in a conceptualization of addiction as a universal phenomenon, and thus its categorization in a clinical lexicon and historiography of disease classifications. Room's particular focus on the sociological "constructionist" thinking places a larger importance on the experiential reality of addiction, and thus the subjective first-person accounts of individual perspectives on addiction serve to further distinguish it from transcultural and more universal normative approaches to the categorization of addiction as a physiological, and thus medically observable, disease.

> In the context of that movement, [...] drinking came into focus as a potential explanation of bad events or behavior. Americans came to see alcohol as an exceptionally powerful substance that not only made drinkers clumsy but also made them behave in ways in which they would not wish to behave when sober. Once the connection of drinking or drug use to bad behavior and events is made, this becomes a powerful two-fold argument against drinking or drug use and for the user to give up such use. [...] Once the drinker could be taught the error of his ways, he would give up what he must now recognize as noxious behavior.
>
> (Room, 1985, para. 7,8)

In this perspective, we can begin to see the emergence of "harm" as a focal point, one which will be central to the ethical claim of this book. A harmful behaviour, addiction becomes an intrinsically wrongful practice that must be tempered (whether through coercion, nudging, or simply individual self-restraint). Room further argues that the very failure of the drinker to cease this "harmful behavior" is what gives birth to the modern conception of addiction, i.e. the inability to stop a practice which causes oneself and others harm. In the modern clinical definition, within the International Classification of Diseases, 10th Revision (ICD-10; World Health Organization 2004), as well as the Diagnostic and Statistical Manual of the American Psychiatric Association, 5th edition (5th ed., DSM–5; American Psychiatric Association, 2013), the criteria for defining addiction as a disease include the notion of continued use despite knowledge of its harmful consequences.

Indeed, although the consumption of psychoactive substances may be as old as civilization itself (Guerra-Doce, 2015), Room and others argue that the notion of a certain type of substance, or rather a certain type of consumers of such substances, being a problem for society dates to the beginning of the industrial age and its effect on the conception of the citizen within the Liberal State (Seddon, 2010). This problematization of the consumption of psychoactive substances emerged, according to Room's view, from having to conciliate the paradox of a need for sobriety in the new mechanical practices that represented the majority of the workforce's occupations upon the advent of the Industrial Revolution, with the economic need for the substances to be widely consumed as part of the commodities trade upon which most colonial empires were built (alcohol, tobacco, tea, opium, chocolate, and sugar) (Room, 2006). According to Toby Seddon, in the context of the Industrial Revolution, the notion of freedom in the philosophically *liberal* sense made of addiction, its conceptual opposite, an intrinsically liberal problem. As Seddon argues:

> At the heart of the liberal imaginary was the idea of individual freedom. Maximizing the liberty of citizens, and placing limits on the power of the state, was seen as one of the principal purposes of liberal government. The liberal subject was, accordingly, understood as a more or less autonomous individual capable of exercising free will.
>
> (Seddon, 2010, p. 9)

This problematization of addiction then makes of addiction a social problem to be solved through regulation. The argumentative structure of this book will follow this lead, establishing first a philosophical understanding of addiction, contrasting a neuroreductionist modelization of addiction as a brain disease, in order to finally coalesce the discussion in the realm of policy construction and their ethical implications.

In other words, and without trying to sound obtuse, problematizing addiction is in large part the problem. It is indeed a seemingly intractable social, and cross-cutting phenomenon whose solution may take the form of individual choice all the way up to geopolitical decisions by national governments and international committees, but one that emerges nonetheless from our very specific social and cultural history. Yet, for all the attention the problem has garnered in the last century and up to the present day, it is one of the areas with the least visible progress in public policy. Aside from punctual and very specific strategies to curb the emergence of the HIV/AIDS epidemic at the end of the 20th century (Berridge, 1996), the state of addiction and drug policy is in more or less the same ideological place today as it was 50 years ago. Few other areas have shown such little headway into making a solution seem at least visible, a situation wherein addiction could hold the same space in the collective unconscious as any other physical/mental disease. What is more, even fewer areas of social and political issues receive the kind of mediatic attention, political discourse, and social debate as to the nature of the phenomenon and the best approach to solving it. It is perhaps this very multiplicity of dimensions intrinsic to the notion of addiction that can provide an answer as to the best approach to dealing with it. This book will operate under the guiding principle that an analysis of addiction drawing on multiple perspectives may provide new understandings that would help indicate possible solutions to this multifaceted problem.

Argumentative Structure

The motivation for this book is to deal with the sociopolitical problem of addiction to illicit psychoactive substances. More specifically, it aims to deal with the ethical concern of how policies conceive of and treat addicted persons, considering what we may know about the nature of addiction. As I mentioned at the beginning of this introduction, I will be breaking down such a question into its thematic components, beginning with the philosophical notion of "addiction". What does it mean to be addicted?

The latest edition of the Diagnostic and Statistical Manual of Mental Disorders (DSM-5, 2013) provides a clinical definition of substance-related disorders in the following manner:

> The substance-related disorders encompass 10 separate classes of drugs: alcohol; caffeine; cannabis; hallucinogens (with separate categories for phencyclidine [or similarly acting arylcyclohexylamines] and other hallucinogens); inhalants; opioids; sedatives, hypnotics, and anxiolytics; stimulants (amphetamine-type substances, cocaine, and other stimulants); tobacco; and other (or unknown) substances. These 10 classes are not fully distinct. All drugs that are taken in excess have in common direct activation of the brain reward system, which is involved in the reinforcement of behaviors and the production of memories. They produce such an intense activation of the reward system that normal activities may be neglected. Instead of achieving reward system activation through adaptive behaviors, drugs of abuse directly activate the reward pathways. The pharmacological mechanisms by which each class of drugs produces reward are different, but the drugs typically activate the system and produce feelings of pleasure, often referred to as a "high." Furthermore, individuals with lower levels of self-control, which may reflect impairments of brain inhibitory mechanisms, may be particularly predisposed to develop substance use disorders, suggesting that the roots of substance use disorders for some persons can be seen in behaviors long before the onset of actual substance use itself.
>
> (DSM-5, 2013)

Already, such a definition contains complex phenomenological concepts, such as "self-control", and the definition itself points to the underlying roots of the disorder that may be present before the consumption of the substance in question. Therefore, the foundation of our understanding of addiction cannot only be its clinical definition. Indeed, the DSM-5 itself mobilizes an interdisciplinary approach to the understanding of addiction:

> The essential feature of a substance use disorder is a cluster of cognitive, behavioral, and physiological symptoms indicating that the individual continues using the substance despite significant substance-related problems.
>
> (DSM-5, 2013)

This clinical definition touches on the key philosophical aspect of addiction and the paradoxical nature of addictive behaviour: continued use despite negative consequences. Why, indeed, does a person continue consuming a substance if said consumption has a negative impact on their life? A neurobiological understanding of the underlying mechanisms of addiction can help us better understand *how* addiction works:

> An important characteristic of substance use disorders is an underlying change in brain circuits that may persist beyond detoxification, particularly in individuals with severe disorders. The behavioral effects of these brain changes may be exhibited in the repeated relapses and intense drug craving when the individuals are exposed to drug-related stimuli. These persistent drug effects may benefit from long-term approaches to treatment. [...] Overall, the diagnosis of a substance use disorder is based on a pathological pattern of behaviors related to use of the substance.
>
> (DSM-5, 2013)

However, this clinical definition leaves a gap in our conceptual understanding of *why* addiction happens in the first place, something that may require a more philosophical approach. Over the course of this book, I will attempt to provide an answer to the question of how addiction ought to be conceptualized from a philosophical perspective, what the advances in neuroscientific research can bring to said conceptualization, and finally what this conceptualization means for the construction of more effective and ethical policy strategies aimed at dealing with addicted persons and drug-related harms. I propose that a bioethical approach is well suited to study the inherently transdisciplinary phenomenon of addiction, with the emerging biopsychosocial view of addiction being the most adapted paradigm view of addiction, and which must form the basis of research into addiction and the development of legal and political strategies for the treatment of addicted persons moving forward, negotiating between the benefit of the legitimization of addiction as a medical condition, with the pitfalls of neuroreductionist thinking and the undermining of the complexity of a phenomenon such as addiction.

It is within this bioethical approach that I situate the argument in this book, within the school of thought that recognizes the complexity of addiction as a multifaceted phenomenon, and considers free choice and moral responsibility within the neurobiological, social experience and political and historical context of the society in which the individuals find themselves. With that in mind, I will build the argument in this book along the following structure:

1. *Developing the philosophical concepts of agency and action in the context of addiction*

Firstly, I will situate the sociopolitical context for my bioethical approach in Chapter 1. Here, I will provide an overview of the state of the art concerning the literature and field of study of addiction and specifically evidence-based drug policy as influenced by emerging concepts of addiction. I will lay out what I consider to be the potentially original contribution of my book, i.e. that in social and public health policy analysis, the inclusion of a philosophical and neuroscientific perspective is not only beneficial but necessary in order to make effective and ethical policy recommendations.

Having laid this groundwork, the focus for Chapter 2 will be to develop a theoretical framework for the understanding of a particular kind of agency in the context of addiction. In discussing the ontology of what an addicted action is, I will draw on the standard concept and theory of action, as it has developed in analytic philosophy within the second half of the 20th century. The purpose of this will be to lay the foundation necessary to better incorporate such a philosophical concept into the strategies of harm reduction aimed at dealing with addiction in policy discussions.

Patterns of behaviour, agency, and related concepts of free will, volition, and self-control will thus be needed to understand addiction from a phenomenological perspective and better address the question of "What does it mean to be addicted?" This philosophical enterprise in Chapter 2 will be the first phase of the argumentative structure of my book.

I will there address a first preliminary question of my book: "How should we understand agency and action in the context of addictive behaviour?", wherein I will develop a theoretical framework for the understanding of a particular kind of agency in the context of addiction.

This philosophical foundation is the first entryway into the paradox of addictive behaviour: addicted persons continuing to engage in a behaviour and/or consume a substance which they are aware is detrimental to their health and wellbeing. The philosophical concept at the core of this question being that of agency, I will work on questions of "diminished agency" and how they underlie our moral attitudes towards addicted persons: "Why do they make the wrong choice?" I posit that starting with a philosophical account of agency in the study of addiction must necessarily come before addressing neuroscientific research into the nature and aetiology of addiction as a disorder: "If it isn't a choice, what makes them compelled to act as if it were?" Additionally, this foundation must also be laid before addressing the political debates surrounding addiction as a social phenomenon requiring policy solutions: "How best do we deal with and/or treat people making such detrimental choices, regardless of whether or not it is they who make them?"

I will heavily rely on Donald Davidson's "Actions, reasons and causes" and its stance defending the positivist relationship between language and thoughts/actions. This causal theory of both action and its consequent explanation communicated by the agent, i.e. its rationalization, is the foundation of what would become the standard conception of agency in the philosophy of mind and action, the "belief-desire" model of motivation which frames a lot of contemporary literature on the philosophy of addiction.

With that in mind, the reason I will draw on Donald Davidson's theory of action as applied to the special context of addictive behaviour is the relation between linguistic descriptions of action and their place in an ontology of action, i.e. how propositional logic can be the foundation for first-order logic in an attempt to codify language surrounding action.

I will be situating this section of my book within the field of contemporary philosophical works on addiction and related concepts. This field includes such concepts as the notion of ego depletion as a viable way of understanding why addicted persons seem to feel "compelled" to certain actions (Levy, 2011); whether the different conceptions of "compulsion" are indeed useful in our understanding of addiction (Heather, 2017); the notion of irresistibility in self-control accounts of addiction (Mele, 1996); and what the ancient Greek concept of "akrasia" can tell us about weakness of will in modern-day conceptions of addiction (May & Holton, 2012).

2. *Analyzing the neuroscience of addiction, the ensuing Brain Disease Model and what it can and cannot tell us about the nature of addicted persons' agency*

Having established an account of agency from which to understand the way in which addiction represents a compromised agency, I can then turn to a neuroscientific perspective of addiction. The reason for this is the underlying motivation for a better understanding of addiction: a medicalized view of addiction. A more ethical treatment requires an ontological shift in perspective from addiction as a behavioural disorder to addiction as a medical condition. This needs to be supported by a neuroscientific conceptualization of addiction, and the implications that such conceptual shifts will carry. The second preliminary question that I will address in this part is: "How can a neuroscientific paradigm of addiction illustrate the compromised agency of addicted persons?"

This will be the focus of Chapter 3, which will first present a review of the latest developments in the neuroscience of addiction, in order to critically assess the paradigm known as the brain disease model of addiction (BDMA) and then provide a discussion of the dialogue between the philosophical foundation of compromised agency established in Chapter 2 and said neuroscientific paradigm. The purpose of this chapter will be to present a transdisciplinary methodology of conceptualizing the disorder from which addicted persons suffer. This will in turn help situate the moral framework from which I will critique and review the policies geared towards drug-related harms in the United Kingdom and how they affect addicted persons.

In Chapter 3, I will give a brief summary of how the neuroscientific perspective on addiction came to be shaped, specifically how it has coalesced into the BDMA, how this paradigmatic shift came into being through the research efforts of the National Institute on Drug Abuse (NIDA), and how this view of addictive behaviour understood as a consequence of the "hijacking" of a person's neurocircuitry has come to be the predominant conceptualization of addiction in the clinical literature. In focusing on the paradigmatic aspect of the BDMA, I will explore the relationship between a neuroscientific consensus and the policy construction efforts of NIDA, and see whether there is a feedback loop in the establishment of such a paradigm that can compromise the epistemological value of a scientific model when it comes to be considered politically and socially useful.

I will also try to untangle some of the debate between the neuroscientific perspective on the underlying mechanisms of addictive behaviour and the philosophical understanding of the causal theory of action in the special context of addiction. My discussion will attempt to show how neuroscientific research necessarily mobilizes concepts such as free will, compulsive behaviour, and the nature of a disease, all of which can benefit greatly from a philosophical foundation. Simultaneously, I will argue that a philosophical inquiry into the nature of action and addictive behaviour equally benefits from a solid understanding of the data and empirical knowledge provided by neuroscientific advances.

This chapter will focus on the relationship between the concepts I unpacked in the second chapter dedicated to the philosophical account of addictive actions. Secondly, having already spent some time in the second chapter going over the elemental notions of action and intentionality, I will be looking at specific points of confusion regarding the nature of a "free human action" that can arise in certain areas of neuroscientific literature, the most famous of these, and by far the most contentious, being the Libet experiments (Libet et al., 1983), which claimed to demonstrate that human action was not under conscious control. I will provide a more concrete application of this exchange of disciplinary viewpoints to the case of addicted persons, addressing the temptation to resolve the problem of addiction with clear-cut neuroreductionist evidence that negates all control that an addicted person may have over their behaviour.

The objective of this chapter, and its importance within the broader scope of the book, is to look at the history of how the brain disease paradigm came to be shaped, first by specific scientific advances and discoveries, and then by sociopolitical evolutions in discourse. My hope is to shed a broader light on the ethical implications of the effects that a neurocentric view can have on the political attitude towards a human behavioural problem, how it can alter the course of a societal phenomenon being observed and as such shape the data being used to construct the policies aimed at resolving it. I will argue that a more complex understanding of addiction that avoids simplistic and absolutist answers will be able to provide a more ethical account of responsibility for addicted persons.

3. *Reviewing the criminal law account of addicted persons' responsibility, its effect on UK drug policy strategies, and assessing whether a Harm Reduction strategy can be better suited to the treatment of addicted persons in society*

This will be the focus of Chapters 4 and 5, which will first lay out the account of criminal responsibility within which drug policy has been constructed over the past century, and then provide a critical assessment of the ethics and effectiveness of said drug policies. The purpose of this will be to establish a foundation for the normative claim of my book, which is that drug policy construction in the UK has created greater harm to addicted persons than their purported objective of protecting society (including those suffering from addiction) from drug-related harm.

The third and final preliminary question of my book is: "How ought addicted persons be treated in society?" and it concerns the social and political aspects of said treatment. Having laid the philosophical foundation for an understanding of addicted persons' compromised agency, and having subsequently confronted that view with the neuroscientific paradigm of addiction as a brain disease, the discussion will then focus on what public health policy strategies are better suited to dealing with addicted persons' compromised agency and responsibility. Exploring this question will allow me to bring together the previous sections of my book and address the ethical question of how addicted persons ought to be treated from a policy standpoint, in view of a philosophically sound understanding of their compromised agency and the supporting neuroscientific evidence of their condition.

Chapter 4 will attempt to provide a critical and ethical analysis of the conceptual basis that underlies the UK drug policy framework, by reviewing the conceptual basis for a criminal law approach to drug control, and assessing the sociopolitical impact that these policies have had in the scene of substance abuse in the United Kingdom. I will start by looking at the law's conception of responsibility and consider the attitude that the law has and ought to have towards compulsivity and/or mitigating excuses that challenge the normal presumption of intentionality in criminal acts. I will offer some thoughts on the ethical considerations related to harm reduction that are needed for proposed legal and policy reforms aimed at ameliorating the justice system's approach to dealing with addicted persons convicted of drug-related crimes.

Chapter 5 will present the argument of my book concerning UK drug policy strategies and the ethical analysis of the different constructs employed in building said policies. Having spent some time in Chapter 4 overlooking the history of drug policy in the United Kingdom, specifically a narrative of legislative events that culminate in the development of "harm reduction" strategies, I will then discuss what I call the "Difference in Effectiveness in Harm Reduction", a distinction between two types of policy construction frameworks, "External to Local" (E-L) and "Local to External" (L-E), providing arguments for their varying levels of effectiveness in reducing the societal harms of addiction. The distinguishing factor is based on the point of origin and direction that a policy construction takes. External policies come from international conventions and are trickled down into local policy (e.g., UN Schedule classifications resulting in local prohibition of substances), while local policies originate from local initiatives and grow outwards to greater size until they are noticed in international arenas (e.g., "harm reduction" strategies like safe injecting rooms which garner notice and are then implemented internationally). These two policy construction frameworks help to situate UK drug policy in the broader context of the international drug control conventions and treaties to which it is beholden as a member of the United Nations, these treaties being the Single Convention on Narcotic Drugs (1962), as amended by the 1972 Protocol; the Convention on Psychotropic Substances (1971); and the Convention Against Illicit Traffic in Narcotic Drugs and Psychotropic Substances (1988).

I will argue that the difference between policy-construction frameworks comes from the epistemological dissonance in their philosophical conception of addiction and specifically the behaviour of addicted persons. I will propose that a traditional view of addicted persons as agents making irrational choices is an erroneous philosophical conception of the addicted person's condition and is at the root of the difference in the effectiveness of policy constructs dealing with addiction.

Ethical Claim

In considering why addiction and addiction-related problems are a worthwhile area of study, it is perhaps easiest to begin with the fact that they represent a significant cost to society. First and foremost, in measuring the harms that can be derived from addiction and drug abuse, the death toll from overdoses represents the ultimate cost of life and a concrete measurable way in which societies may track the progress of their battle against addiction. While a net zero loss of life due to overdose may be a utopic objective, an increase or decrease in the number of overdose deaths per year is one way in which the harm of addiction, and the progress to attenuate that harm, can be tallied.

Secondly, addiction-related health problems represent a terrible toll on the individual suffering from them, and the incurring medical costs represent yet another tangible way of measuring the harm of addiction to a population. Once again, the objective of a perfectly healthy society, free of all addictions and vices, free of all ills and diseases, may not be a realistic one. However, the "health" of a society, and the cost of keeping a society healthy, is a measurable harm that can be tracked and measured in average national public health markers and the financial burdens associated with them.

Finally, drug-related crimes and illicit activities represent an additional burden to society, firstly through the direct harms of violence and death that are correlated to the illicit drug marketplace, and secondly through the implicit cost of policing and incarceration that the State needs to allocate to combat the problem of drug-related crime. This cost may be on a local scale, where police forces are occupied with regional and community level drug dealers; or it may be on a grander scale, where entire subsections of military forces must be directed towards the so-called "War on Drugs" which cross national boundaries and implicate an entire set of geopolitical considerations.

All in all, the harms and costs of addiction represent a truly multidimensional set of problems, thus requiring an equally multidisciplinary approach to solving them. This, of course, also serves to contain the magnitude and scope of any one attempt to address the harms of addiction. This work (or any work, for that matter) cannot attempt to solve the entire set of problems or harms derived from addiction. Rather, it will focus on one specific aspect through which these problems may be tackled: public health policy; and more specifically, harm reduction strategies aimed at shaping policy related to drug consumption and addiction. This book will be taking a bioethical approach to the question it will attempt to answer, beginning with a philosophical foundation of conceptual backgrounds for what we understand to be intentional versus compulsive behaviour in the context of an addiction, providing a review of neurobiological insights into the inner workings of the addicted person's brain, and finally converging into a policy discussion about the ethical implications of our governance and regulation structures meant to deal with the problem of addiction in society.

Therefore, and because of the focus on harm reduction as the main ethical claim of this book, a certain set of value judgements will be present in my discussion, and the measurable ways to solve the "problem" of addiction that have already been mentioned will be assessed through this ethical lens of harm reduction, evaluating the treatment and implications that such policy strategies actually mean for addicted persons. In this sense, the assessment of a particular philosophical view on addicted actions, the implications of a model of addiction that may reduce the lived experience of an addicted person to a neurochemical reaction, and the long-term consequences of a public health policy aimed at dealing with the "problem" of drugs and addiction in society, will be done not only from a purely quantifiable measure of deaths and cost of healthcare but also, and primarily so, through the measure of its ethical value according to notions of social justice and the primacy of individual liberty. Through this ethical lens, and particularly when talking about the socio-political sense of the addiction phenomenon, what I will be discussing is really the problem of how to govern addicted persons in an ethical way. Considering the ethical considerations of the conceptualization of the addiction problem, which entails a broader notion of harm than those that quantifiable metrics can provide, I will argue that a new approach to UK drug policy is needed from an ethical standpoint.

I will propose that harm reduction strategies in policy constructions are more effective in reducing the harm of addiction, as well as being more ethical, because they incorporate a neuroscience-based comprehension of addiction as a disorder which affects the person's ability to coherently form intentional actions, while the type of policy that operates with an outdated rationalist view of addicted persons imposes dissuasive and punitive measures which do not address the underlying disorder of addiction and are thus less effective at reducing the harms of addiction and treat addicted persons in an ethically problematic way.

References

American Psychiatric Association. (2013). Substance-Related and Addictive Disorders. In *Diagnostic and Statistical Manual of Mental Disorders* (5th ed.). https://doi.org/10.1176/appi.books.9780890425596

Berridge, V. (1996). *AIDS in the U.K.: The Making of Policy 1981–1994*. Oxford University Press.

Buchman, D.Z., Skinner, W., & Illes, J. (2010). Negotiating the Relationship Between Addiction, Ethics, and Brain Science. *AJOB Neuroscience*, *1*(1), 36–45.

Guerra-Doce, E. (2015). Psychoactive Substances in Prehistoric Times: Examining the Archaeological Evidence. *Time and Mind*, *8*(1), 91–112. https://doi.org/10.1080/1751696X.2014.993244

Heather, N. (2017). Is the Concept of Compulsion Useful in the Explanation or Description of Addictive Behaviour and Experience? *Addictive Behaviors Reports*, *6*, 15–38. https://doi.org/10.1016/j.abrep.2017.05.002

Levine, H.G. (1978). The Discovery of Addiction. Changing Conceptions of Habitual Drunkenness in America. *Journal of Studies on Alcohol*, *39*(1), 143–174. https://doi.org/10.15288/jsa.1978.39.143

Levy, N. (2011). Addiction, Responsibility, and Ego Depletion. In J. Poland & G. Graham (Eds.), *Addiction and Responsibility* (pp. 89–112). The MIT Press. https://doi.org/10.7551/mitpress/9780262015509.003.0004

Leshner, A.I. (1997). Addiction is a Brain Disease, and it Matters. *Science*, *278*(5335), 45–47.

Libet, B., Libet, B., Gleason, C.A., Wright, E.W., & Pearl, D.K. (1983). Time of Conscious Intention to Act in Relation to Onset of Cerebral Activity (Readiness-Potential). *Brain*, *106*(3), 623–642.

May, J., & Holton, R. (2012). What in the World is Weakness of Will? *Philosophical Studies*, *157*(3), 341–360. https://doi.org/10.1007/s11098-010-9651-8

Mele, A.R. (1996). Addiction and Self-Control. *Behavior and Philosophy*, *24*(2), 99–117. JSTOR.

Room, R. (1985). Dependence and Society. *British Journal of Addiction*, *80*(2), 133–139. https://doi.org/10.1111/j.1360-0443.1985.tb03263.x

Room, R. (2006). Addiction Concepts and International Control. *The Social History of Alcohol and Drugs*, *21*(2), 276–289.

Rosenthal, R.J., & Faris, S.B. (2019). The Etymology and Early History of 'Addiction.' *Addiction Research & Theory*, *27*(5), 437–449. https://doi.org/10.1080/16066359.2018.1543412

Seddon, T. (2010). *A History of Drugs: Drugs and Freedom in the Liberal Age*. Routledge, Taylor & Francis Group. https://books.google.ch/books?id=a-Cg0Ix-qn4C

United Nations Conference for the Adoption of a Single Convention on Narcotic Drugs. (1962). *Single Convention on Narcotic Drugs, 1961*. United Nations.

United Nations. (1971). *Convention on Psychotropic Substances 1971*, 1019 UNTS 175. United Nations.

United Nations. (1988). *Convention Against the Illicit Traffic in Narcotic Drugs and Psychotropic Substances 1988*. UN Doc. E/CONF.82/15, reprinted in 28 ILM 493. United Nations.

World Health Organization. (2004). *ICD-10: International Statistical Classification of Diseases and Related Health Problems: Tenth Revision* (2nded.). World Health Organization.

Chapter 1

Why Addiction is a Bioethical Issue

A Bioethical Approach to the Study of the Addiction Problem

An underlying driving principle of this book will be that addiction as a concept can be analyzed through a bioethical lens, something which requires us to confront the conception of the "addiction problem" and its underlying assumption regarding the way we collectively view the issue of our relationship with psychoactive substances: that it is a unitary phenomenon and not a collection of interrelated social, cultural, economic, and political realities that can converge into a somewhat observable phenomenon that can be labelled "the drug problem".

In that regard, and though obvious to most researchers and people interested in the issue of drugs and addiction, it bears repeating that the "problem" of addiction and its derived social and political dilemmas are multifaceted, cut across various strata of societal life and thus can be observed and analyzed through a variety of disciplines. It is not a phenomenon that can adequately and comprehensively be understood through the lens of one singular viewpoint. Yes, understanding the chemical composition of a psychoactive substance will give us a clearer insight into its action on the brain and thus help us better understand what it is that makes it so "addictive" in that sense[1], not to mention it will help us better understand its subsequent metabolic journey through the human body, thus helping us better understand the physiological risks of continuous use of said substance. But the chemical composition of a psychoactive substance is not the only lens through which we can understand addiction.

Indeed, the neuroscientific understanding of what goes on in the brain is crucial to understanding a certain aspect of the addiction process, though it gets us no closer to understanding why a person decides to consume the substance in the first place or after a long period of recovery, leading to relapse. For that, we need to incorporate a psychological understanding of the pain, suffering, and anxiety that often leads a person to consume drugs in the first place. In this psychological realm, the "addictive" aspect of a substance will be

DOI: 10.4324/9781003582908-2

its ability to numb the pain or dull the senses for long enough for a person to feel some measure of relief from their anxiety and suffering, oftentimes brought about from childhood trauma (Maté, 2012). It is in this realm that we begin to speak of things like "addictive personalities" and begin to see the comorbidity with other types of mental illnesses and disorders (Volkow, 2001).

Broadening out our perspective even further, the social conditions and environments within which addicted persons grow up and live in are yet another area of study, integral to a holistic understanding of the problem of addiction in society. Sociological and historico-political perspectives are thus needed in painting a more detailed picture of what addiction is as a social phenomenon, and how we can best resolve it through governance. Here, considerations of market price fluctuations, offer and demand, availability of product, and cheaper alternatives (oftentimes more harmful), begin to emerge. This leads us to the social and political disciplines that deal with domestic and international geopolitics, and the various narratives that are constructed to shape policy-making decisions with regards to dealing with substance abuse problems in a population, rather than the individual.

But the problem of addiction is not only multidisciplinary, i.e. it can be studied from multiple perspectives; it is inherently interdisciplinary, i.e. those disciplines need to be in dialogue with one another in order to get the full picture. Hence the need for not only a multiplicity of perspectives to be brought to the table to fully understand the problem, but also a need for those perspectives to feed into each other in order to construct a methodology that is adequate for solving the problem.

In addition to being an interdisciplinary problem, addiction as a bioethical issue is concerned with the ethical implications of the policies dealing with addicted persons. At the heart of the problem of addiction, from an individual perspective, is the notion of choice, of voluntary action, and ultimately of free will. Do we have the capacity to overcome an irresistible urge and craving through sheer force of will and motivation? Or are the chemical forces at play in our brain so overwhelming that no amount of resolve can withstand them? How can we best understand these notions of action and volition, to better comprehend the specific instances of substance consumption and the cravings associated with it? Finally, how should these inquiries into the philosophical realm of causal action and free will affect our attitudes towards addicted persons, and more importantly how ought they translate into more ethical and fair policies around the "drug problem"?

The need for an interdisciplinary methodology to the study of the addiction problem comes from the inherent tension in the ways we understand and try to solve it, depending on which disciplinary lens we look through. At first, it may seem like a purely criminological issue to ask how a society can solve its drug problem. A balance of proper social security measures, healthy social conditions, and tempered State enforcement will most likely present itself as the solution.

If, on the other hand, one attempts to understand addiction from a more individual perspective, i.e. "how does a person fall into an addiction?", the path to answering that question will take a different disciplinary route. From a purely mechanical perspective, one can look at neuroscience to provide the answer to the question of "how?" Indeed, a look at the underlying mechanisms of neurons, neuronal synapses, and the activation of dopamine pathways in the central nervous system will paint a fairly clear picture of what addiction looks like from a molecular level, i.e. how it works. This level of understanding may then inform treatment methods, as well as potentially more robust information campaigns regarding the dangers of drug consumption.

This, however, gets us no nearer to answering the question of why addiction happens in the first place. Nor does it present a realistic pathway to solving the sociopolitical reality of addiction rates, overdose deaths, and further public health harms, as well as economic costs related to addiction in society. And it is perhaps this final note, regarding the unknowability and complexity of this phenomenon that accentuates the interdisciplinary nature of the addiction problem. It is indeed difficult to envision any kind of society in which all people consume every single substance in the proper amount, and that every single one of those substances is a net-health-positive one (e.g., no refined sugar or alcohol). It is even more difficult to imagine any conceivable method of governance which would get us any way nearer to that utopic reality, without descending into very dystopic realms of authoritarian overreach. Indeed, some of the very institutions dedicated to the combat against drugs in society are conscious of its intractable nature as a problem. The Executive Director of the United Nations Office on Drugs and Crime made the following remarks during a speech in 2007:

> Is a drugs free world attainable? Probably not. Is it desirable? Most certainly, yes. Therefore, I see this slogan as an aspirational goal, and not as an operational target – in the same way that we all aspire to eliminate poverty, hunger, illiteracy, diseases, even wars.
>
> (Costa, 2007)

Curiously, in that same speech, Costa mentioned:

> [...] we can all agree on the need to reduce the harm caused by drugs -- by preventing their use, by treating those who abuse them, and by limiting the damage they cause to the individual and society. [...] I hope we also agree on the need to ensure that drug policy is evidence-based, not the result of political considerations or ideological preferences.
>
> (Costa, 2007)

This concern with the "harms" of the addiction problem reinforces the fact that the ethical focus needs to be defined as the treatment and consideration of the persons who directly suffer from addiction. Correlated to that concern is the broader context of their place in society and the harms that can be associated with drug abuse. This brings us to questions of how policies ought to address those harms in an ethical manner. The conciliation of harm reduction with a respect for the autonomy of individuals dealing with addiction is one key aspect of the bioethical concern over paternalistic and condescending attitudes in a clinical setting as well as the harsh punitive measures applied to deal with drug-related crimes. The primary ethical concern of reducing harm, in any shape that harm may take (e.g., overdose deaths, chronic mental suffering, deterioration of the social environment, drug-related crime, etc.), is the guiding value behind a bioethical approach to dealing with addiction.

State of the Art

This book will look at different disciplinary fields of research into addiction (philosophy of addiction, neuroscience of addiction, and drug policy), and as such it will have to situate itself within various fields of literature and contemporary discussions.

Current debates in the bioethics of addiction

The current state of the bioethical discussion on addiction is intrinsically linked to the Brain Disease Model of Addiction (BDMA), which will feature heavily in this book and will serve as a starting point for a deeper analysis of the neuroscience of addiction and its ethical implications on our conceptualizations of it, as I will describe in the following section. But aside from the details of the neuroscience of addiction, it is the general medicalization of addiction that is at the heart of many of the current debates on addiction in bioethics: the implied promise of a more effective (i.e., medical) treatment of addiction through neuroactive medication, the consequences in the collective unconscious of an oversimplified concept and its effects in popular discourse, and the inclusion of addiction treatment in health insurance coverage.

Another one of the purported benefits of the BDMA would be the normalization of addiction via its destigmatization, a view that has been challenged, either by concepts of "responsibility without blame" that attempt to conciliate the accountability necessary in assigning responsibility to addicted persons for their choices, without the moral castigation usually associated with it (Pickard, 2017) or "compassionate choice models of addiction" that seek to find empathy and understanding of the high degree of difficulty in overcoming addictive impulses, without denying the active choice involved in addictive actions (Clark, 2021).

That very notion of choice, and in a bioethical sense the notion of the "autonomy" that can be exhibited by an individual, is a core component of the debate around the nature of addiction. To what extent can the autonomy of an individual be undermined if they are under the influence of mind-altering substances and therefore demonstrate a compromised sense of agency?

These questions in essence revolve around the same ontological question of "what is addiction?" Is it a mental disorder that absolves liability for one's actions? This relates to a more specific field of legal theory and debate on the responsibility of addicted persons when committing drug-related crimes (Morse, 2003). Is it a clinically observable condition, which ought to be conceived of and treated (with all the implied political support for healthcare attributed to it) via a medical approach? Is it a consequence of disrupted neurocircuitry and as such a disorder on a par, ontologically and with regards to blameworthiness, with other neurodegenerative diseases such as Parkinson's or Alzheimer's disease?

The multifaceted nature of the addiction problem means that there is not only one bioethical problem when it comes to addiction. And it will be beyond the scope of my book to address every facet of the bioethical debate surrounding addiction. Indeed, this book will exclude other compulsive behaviours (e.g., gambling, sex addiction, internet addiction, etc.) that can very well fall under the conceptualization of addiction, and which can share modelizations of dopamine-related disrupted neurocircuitry as a causal explanation for their disorder. Each of these other disorders can be its own area of study and has a space dedicated to it in the literature on the bioethics of addiction. For the purposes of this book, I will focus on the bioethical questions concerning the relationship between public health policy constructs and neuroscientific paradigms of understanding addiction to illicit psychoactive substances, and crucially what the ethical implications are of said relationship for the treatment of addicted persons in UK drug policy.

Current state of the neuroscience of addiction

At the core of our current understanding of how drugs affect behaviour are the extraordinary advances that have been made in the field of neuroscience of addiction. We now understand much more about the connectivity of the brain, how its functionality depends on the chemical communication between nerve cells called neurons, and how this communication takes the form of neurotransmitters released which then bind to receptors. Psychoactive substances exert their influence on the brain by affecting the regulation of neurotransmitters, particularly dopamine, or by simulating their actions at the receptors. Compounded with our understanding of how different parts of the brain work at a systems level to modulate behaviour and cognitive function, this has led to a much clearer picture of the neurobiological effect of drugs and their long-term consumption.

As mentioned above, the literature on this topic has been largely influenced by the notion that "addiction is a brain disease", a view most prominently championed in the late 1990s by the director of the National Institute for Drug Abuse (NIDA) at the time, Alan Leshner (Leshner, 1997), and which continues to be widely supported in the neuroscientific literature today (Volkow et al., 2016). This has coalesced into what is commonly referred to as the "brain disease model of addiction" (BDMA), and it has gained widespread acceptance in the field of neuroscience as the dominant paradigmatic understanding of addiction. The NIDA continues to be the largest federal research institute on drug abuse and addiction in the United States, and the advances in research since the first introduction into the literature of the BDMA have only bolstered and reinforced the position that the underlying mechanisms of addiction in the brain are tantamount to a disease (Volkow et al., 2016). NIDA covers areas of treatment and prevention of drug abuse based on the latest epidemiological, neurobiological, and behavioural science available. The impact and influence of NIDA is such that the "NIDA paradigm" can be used as a shorthand for the consensus view within the neuroscientific literature that addiction can be best understood as a chronic and relapsing brain disease.

The field of neuroscience research largely must operate in relation to this paradigm, whether they adopt it or are critical of it. Researchers have had to position themselves along this debate either by providing supporting research into specialized areas wherein the BDMA can provide a paradigmatic framework for studies of different kinds of addiction, such as food addiction (Volkow et al., 2017) and sugar addiction (Wiss et al., 2018); or by challenging and contesting the underlying claims of the BDMA from treatment and recovery perspectives, as well as bioethical implications of the neuroreductionism of the BDMA (Heather et al., 2018), to questioning whether the BDMA is indeed supported by the empirical evidence of neurobiological research (Hall et al., 2015). This paradigm is also challenged by ethical analysis of the effect that it has on the stigmatization of addicted persons (Trujols, 2015), its impact on clinical settings (Barnett et al., 2018), and the treatment of vulnerable populations (Evans & Cahill, 2016).

In including the neuroscientific perspective on drug addiction, my intention is by no means to contribute to the neuroscientific field of research, but rather to present the context within which the underlying neurobiological mechanisms of addiction, and what we have come to understand about them, are contrasted with the psychological, social, and environmental aspects of addiction. This contrast is meant to serve as a backdrop to the critical analysis that I will undertake regarding the policy strategies employed to deal with addiction and drug-related crimes. While I cannot pretend to provide an exhaustive review of the entire neuroscientific field of research on addiction, in providing a brief overview of the state of the research, I hope to summarize the general tenets of the most current understanding of the underlying neural mechanisms that characterize addiction as a chronic and relapsing brain disorder. This is because a large part of the policy analysis within which I situate my book is based on both the neuroscientific paradigms of understanding addiction, as well as the legal frameworks that are put in place to address this public health issue. The NIDA paradigm has been largely influential in the political arena, creating both a further de-stigmatization of addicted persons and greater allocation of funds for research and medical treatment options for substance abuse[2], likening it to a mental health disorder and distancing it from the criminal behaviour perspective which had been synonymous with addiction for so long.

This progress in the conception of addiction as a brain disease, however, has not entirely subverted the conception of addicted persons as liable and responsible for their actions from the perspective of criminal justice in case of drug-related crimes. From a criminological perspective, the position that "*… addicts retain sufficient rational and control capacities at the relevant times to be held responsible, especially for crimes that are not part of the definition of addiction itself*" (Morse, 2013) is the dominant legal view and opposes the proposition that addiction ought to be held in the same regard as "legal insanity".

The disconnect between a medicalized view of addiction, and the account of criminal responsibility of addicted persons, points to the inherently interdisciplinary methodology that is required for the study of addiction: a phenomenon which not only can be understood from various disciplinary perspectives but must necessarily involve a dialogue between distinct approaches to solve the ethical dilemma of the treatment of addicted persons. One of the key disciplinary perspectives with which the neuroscience of addiction must contend is the philosophy of addiction.

Current debates on the philosophy of addiction

Though it is always difficult to project onto the future, it can be fair to assume that looking back on the past few decades leading up to our present moment, this era of addiction studies will be described as one where changes in our thinking and conceptualization of addiction occurred, when a paradigmatic shift in the understanding of the aetiology of addiction as a disorder came to be established. The limits of our traditional concepts of addiction can already be glaring in some respects and some overly simple dichotomies, such as the notion of compulsion versus the idea of free will, are beginning to feel dated.

The field of philosophy of addiction touches on fundamental questions about human agency, autonomy, consciousness, and rational action. Some philosophers have already tried to compile the fundamental concepts regarding philosophy and addiction, like Jeffrey Poland and George Graham's "Addiction and Responsibility" (Poland & Graham, 2011), "What is Addiction?" (Ross et al., 2010), and "Addiction and Self-Control: Perspectives from Philosophy, Psychology and Neuroscience" (Levy, 2012). These compilations attempt to provide an overview of the various concepts at work in the field of addiction studies.

Many philosophers, like Bennett Foddy, Edmund Henden, Jeanette Kennett, and Neil Levy, show that the philosophy of addiction cannot be so easily dissociated from the advances in scientific understandings of addiction and that these two fields of study are part of a continuum of our comprehension of this multidimensional phenomenon, and as such are mutually dependent on one another. This is even more evident when research projects bring together philosophers and neuroscientists to work on certain ideas and concepts, like Richard Holton and Kent Berridge's "Addiction: between compulsion and choice" (Holton & Berridge, 2013), which attempts to re-think addictive cravings and the moral evaluations we derive from their conception, carving a middle ground between the two extreme positions of a pure choice model and a neuroreductionist brain disease model; and Hanna Pickard and Serge Ahmed who collaborated on an attempt to provide a scientific hypobook based on rat experiments to the philosophical dilemma of why addicted persons routinely choose to continue to use despite negative consequences, and why this animal research could provide insights into the nature of human addiction (Pickard & Ahmed, 2016). These intersections between the philosophy and the science of addiction are at the centre of most contemporary discussions over the conceptualization of addiction (Pickard & Ahmed, 2019).

My book contains within it a philosophical inquiry, a question of epistemological and phenomenological concern ("What is the experience of addiction?" and "How best should we understand this phenomenon?"), as well as one of ethical concerns ("How ought addicted persons be treated?"). The philosophical literature with which I engage to build the argumentative structure of my book therefore concerns very specific questions of human action.

In order to construct an account of agency from which to understand the compromised nature of action in the context of addiction, I work within the literature on the philosophy of action. An entire review of the philosophy of action is far beyond the scope of my book, for such a project could be tantamount to a review of the history of Western philosophy, from pre-socratic philosophers to modern-day scholars. As such, I have mainly focused my research on works on the ontological and conceptual issues concerning the nature of action, its relation to events (not least the movements of our bodies), and our descriptions of them, all within the context of addiction or at least with a relevant conceptual framework within which those concepts can be framed within the study of addiction. In this regard, I have engaged with works by E. J. Lowe and Wayne A. Davis, both of whom touch on the ontology of action and the philosophy of mind as related to action.

The broader field of free will and determinism as a philosophical debate has to be included in the body of literature that I mention, mainly because ideas of addiction as a case study of neurobiological determinism reference those notions. As such, though I will not engage directly with the works on free will by Alfred R. Mele, John F. Fischer, and Daniel Dennett, they form the broader environment of philosophical debate within which are situated the specific dilemmas on addiction with which I engage.

Another area of the literature, and more specific to the ideas of agency and causation, includes works on philosophical thought centred around the production, purpose, and explanation of action, motivation, and deliberation. These authors include G. E. M. Anscombe and Donald Davidson, whose works expressly reference each other and respond to one another's views on action, justification of action, and the rationalization of action.

Specific authors, whose work directly relates to addiction and compulsion, and agential causation with regard to addictive behaviour, include Neil Levy, Hanna Pickard, and Edmund Henden. Their work deals with notions of compulsion, the contrast between different disciplinary perspectives on the nature of addiction, and the contextualization of self-control (and lack thereof) as a defining feature of addiction. I engage with the notions presented in their work to contrast them with the neuroreductionist aspects of the BDMA. In that regard, I equally engage with works by philosophers like Nick Heather, Hanna Pickard, and Eddy Nahmias, who specifically deal with the bioethical implications of the BDMA and epistemological questions concerning what neuroscience can tell us about rationality, free will, autonomy, and responsibility.

Current data and trends in drug use and drug-related harm

The primary empirical data on drug statistics in the United Kingdom comes from the Office for National Statistics (ONS), which produces annual reports on drug-related deaths[3], and the European Monitoring Center for Drugs and Drug Addiction (EMCDDA), which places this data in the broader context of the European continent, providing trends and pattern analyses on drug-related deaths and mortality among drug users in Europe[4]. These organizations provide large sets of data and epidemiological indicators based on national, population-based statistics on deaths and harms directly attributable to the use of drugs, as well as estimations of the general and cause-specific mortality rates among drug users. The objective of these institutions is to provide information that informs policy decisions and measures the impact of said policies after they have been implemented.

My book does not intend to provide more statistical data to this body of literature, nor will it produce second-level statistical analysis based on this data. But it will engage with the literature that analyzes this data and forms its arguments based on the trends and patterns outlined in these reports, and therefore these reports have to be included in the body of literature that I present, as they form the basis for the overall argument that drug policies in the United Kingdom have not been successful in reversing trends of increasing overdose deaths and drug-related harms so far.

The level of analysis at which my book will engage with the data on drug use and drug-related harms is in the policy responses that are constructed to address such societal phenomena, as well as the effect of these policies on drug users' health as a broader type of political, ethical, and sociological analysis. Numerous advocacy groups and voluntary organizations have produced a great deal of research into the harmful and unfair impact that drug policies have had on the population of addicted persons, and my research has largely engaged the publications and conclusions of these organizations. These include:

- The IDHDP (International Doctors for Healthier Drug Policies), a "global network of medical doctors that supports drug policies based on the health of individuals and society";
- Harm Reduction International (HRI), an NGO dedicated to reducing the negative health, social, and legal impacts of drug use and drug policy, with Special Consultative Status with the Economic and Social Council of the United Nations;
- RELEASE, which is a national centre of expertise on drugs and drugs law in the United Kingdom that provides specialist advice and information to the public and policymakers on matters of drug use and drug policy. This organization has promoted and advocated for evidence-based policies based on a public health approach, rather than a criminal justice approach, and also has a Special Consultative Status with the Economic and Social Council of the United Nations;
- The International Drug Policy Consortium (IDPC) is one of the largest global networks of NGOs that focus on issues related to drug production, trafficking, and use. It comprises some of the advocacy groups I've already mentioned and equally has an objective of open debate around issues of effectiveness and impact of drug policies, at both national and international levels.

These networks and organizations share the same core principles of producing and disseminating knowledge and information on issues related to drug policy, with a position of advocacy for harm reduction practices and critical analysis of drug policy. Therefore, there is a large overlap between the authors and members of these organizations, who will oftentimes co-author position papers and research studies, such as the RELEASE and Harm Reduction International's response to the Department of Health and Social Care (DHSC)'s September 2021 Consultation on expanding access to naloxone, which analyzed the DHSC's proposed amending of the Human Medicines Regulations 2012 so that certain services other than drug treatment services could supply naloxone to individuals without a prescription and be supplied at other venues than only pharmacies.[5]

These organizations produce large reports that provide invaluable statistical analysis and overviews of drug-related harms and policy impacts, such as the HRI's "Global State of Harm Reduction"[6] and the International Narcotics

Control Board (INCB) Annual Report of 2021[7]. These reports provide a general overview of the state of policy and policy impact around the world, helping to situate UK drug policy in the broader context of the international drug control conventions and treaties to which it is beholden as a member of the United Nations[8], i.e. the Single Convention on Narcotic Drugs (1961), as amended by the 1972 Protocol; the Convention on Psychotropic Substances (1971); and the Convention Against Illicit Traffic in Narcotic Drugs and Psychotropic Substances (1988).

My book is intended as an addition to this body of literature, from the perspective of policy analysis and critical review of the impact that policy has on addicted persons. The normative values shared by these organizations around the benefits of a harm reduction approach to drug control are in line with my book, and the original contribution that this book will hopefully have is in the presentation of a conceptual framework for the analysis of different policy constructs, with a clear advocation for a policy construct modelled on the view that addiction is a disorder from which a person suffers and which ought to be treated as if it were a medical condition, instead of a criminal offence.

Original Contribution

Though it is by no means an original thought to say that addiction as a phenomenon is inherently multidimensional and that its study requires an interdisciplinary approach, I do presume to make the original point that even within a specific subset of a disciplinary perspective inquiry into addiction, i.e. social policy analysis, the inclusion of a philosophical and neuroscientific perspective in a clearly delineated approach with harm reduction as its guiding principle of policy ethos is not only beneficial but even necessary in order to generate a new type of policy-making with regards to drug consumption and addiction in the 21st century.

To understand what may have been the difficulties in solving this problem so far, it is imperative that we understand the epistemological dissonance within the philosophical conception of addiction, and specifically the behaviour of addicted persons, in the policy-construction frameworks that have not embraced the conception of addiction as a brain disease. The thrust of the philosophical argument behind the BDMA, to the extent that it will be relevant for this book, concerns the classification of addiction as a disorder to be viewed (and treated) clinically, with all the deferment and empathy directed towards any other physiological disease, i.e. immune from social stigmatization and an object of no concern for the criminal justice system.

The section dedicated to the philosophy of action, and more specifically the realm of causal action theory, will provide the necessary conceptual tools to better analyze this dissonance in policy constructs. My book will postulate that a philosophical understanding of the addicted person's experience can be extrapolated to a policy construct aiming to treat addicted persons' behaviour as part of a medical disorder (i.e., a brain disease) and that such an approach is directly linked to harm reduction strategies being more effective in dealing with addiction problems in society.

I will also draw on a legislative historical context as a background for my book argument, for it helps to situate the problem of addiction as a problem of liberal governance. The analysis of UK drug policy in this book will place harm reduction policies as part of a continuum of a historical narrative of legislative events, such as described by Toby Seddon in "*A History of Drugs*" (Seddon, 2009). I will argue that the strategies for locally-originated clinical trials and research projects involving harm reduction approaches to dealing with drug-related harms are the consequence of the historically ineffective punitive measures that have guided UK policy-making around drugs and addiction since the latter part of the 19th century. The sections focusing on the contrast between a philosophical account of agency in addiction and the advances in the neuroscience of addiction will serve to bolster the argument for the utility of said conceptualization of addiction as a brain disease and its place in the distinction between local and external policy constructs aimed at dealing with addiction and drug-related harms.

In doing so, I will be situating my book in the recently-developed "biopsychosocial" approach to addiction policy recommendations (Buchman et al., 2010), which argues that the effectiveness of drug policy constructs depends to some degree upon their philosophical conceptions of addicted persons and their behaviour. Biopsychosocial models offer a more holistic approach to the understanding of addiction and integrate a physiological understanding of the brain mechanisms involved in addiction with a socially conscious contextualization of addiction within a particular economic and political environment. They have become much more prominent in the literature on addiction studies of late and have introduced that perspective into discussions about the policies aimed at dealing with addiction. This book will place itself firmly in that school of thought and will attempt to provide a broader understanding of the link between a neurobiological notion of addiction with an evidence-based approach to constructing harm-reduction policies and thus hopefully contribute to a more ethical treatment of addicted persons in society.

It is in the understanding of the different disciplinary areas that will feed into the biopsychosocial argument that I will construct that my book statement begins to naturally take shape. In summary, my book will be drawing on observations and analyses of different policy strategies aimed at dealing with addiction in the United Kingdom. From this observation, two broad categories of policy constructs emerge: a local one and an external one. The distinguishing factor that separates these two policy constructs is based on the point of origin and direction that it takes. External policies come from an outside-looking-in perspective and establish monolithic views on the nature of addiction and consequently its best method of treatment; they generally trickle down into local policies that reinforce criminalization stances and punitive measures as the best method of dissuasion for addicted persons. Local policies, by contrast, originate from clinical initiatives that attempt to treat the harms of addiction from a health perspective first and grow outwards to greater size until they take on national (and even international) importance and recognition. The ethical argument that results from this distinction is one that favours the treatment of addicted persons as suffering from a medically treatable brain disorder (regardless of its actual reductionist definition as such), in order to reduce both the tangible and intangible harms that result from substance abuse to the individual and society as a whole.

My main postulate is that the latter type of policy is a more ethical method of treating addicted persons and that this is intrinsically linked to the fact it is also a more effective method of reducing the harm of addiction because it incorporates a neuroscientific-based comprehension of addiction as a disorder which affects the person's ability to coherently form intentional actions; while the former type of policy operates with an outdated rationalist view of addicted persons and imposes dissuasive and punitive measures which do not address the underlying disorder of addiction.

Notes on Scope

It may be pertinent here to mention some of the areas and categories of addiction which will not be discussed throughout this book: behavioural addictions (e.g., gambling, sex addiction, internet addiction, etc.). Though neurobiologically the same phenomenon is occurring in the brain when a person consumes heroin as when a person places a bet on a roulette table, we will have to make a distinction between those two scenarios. The distinction comes from various aspects, one being that of different moral judgements. Indeed, the previous two scenarios mentioned do have notable degrees of difference in social stigmatization, even though from a purely neuroreductionist point of view, the process may be seen abstractly as the same. The distinction also comes from a clinical perspective, where we have to recognize a difference based on the physiological consequences of one addiction over another. Though gambling and porn addiction may manifest themselves neurobiologically in a similar manner to smoking tobacco, the physiological ramifications for a person will be quite different. The diagnosis of a substance dependence, its preferred method of treatment, and finally the possibilities of relapse are all factors that distinguish substance abuse disorders amongst themselves, but they at least share the same group trait of being able to be treated clinically.

Additionally, our heuristic moral attitudes towards different types of addiction offer some insight into how we classify them. Though the neurobiological mechanisms may be similar, and though the physiological consequences may distinguish one type of addiction from another, in the end, the distinction I will make is in large part due to the social and political framework through which one addiction is dealt with versus another. After all, addiction specialists will be quick to point out that caffeine is the single largest addictive substance consumed globally every single day, and yet little policy discussion or political effort is put into attempting to dismantle the Starbucks Cartel. So the actual point of distinction may simply be the way in which we view certain addictions as licit and legitimate, with almost no social stigma attached to it; versus the much more stern and concerned view we may take towards the social, economic, and political ramifications of another type of addiction, devoting resources, time, and effort to understanding the neurobiological basis for it, its environmental and natural causality, and ultimately the most appropriate way of ridding society of it. Referring back to the perspective on the problematization of addiction mentioned in the introduction, it is perhaps because of our constructionist view of certain addictions as problems that they indeed become a problem we must devote efforts to solving.

This book will dip its toe into the philosophical pond of addiction as an abstract concept involving free will, the nature of causal action, and the ability of a conscious being to overcome seemingly deterministic neurobiological conditions. However, it is by no means meant to be an exhaustive look into the nature of addiction as an abstract phenomenon of the human condition. I will therefore limit my arguments to the concrete aspects of policy and legal discussions surrounding the matter of substance abuse. By focusing on this type of addiction, I will be able to ground the discussion in detailed neuroscience studies looking at the effect that specific substances can have on the chemical structure of the brain, in specific policy stands involving the control and regulation of said substances and their distribution in society, and finally in the ethical discussion regarding the treatment of persons suffering from a chronic dependence on those substances.

A final note on the specific focus on substance abuse is to make the distinction regarding the influence that policy will have on the actual problem at hand. Indeed, part of the problematization that I will look at is the feedback loop that can occur when criminalization policies will exacerbate an existing social problem of drug abuse. This exacerbating factor happens to be an issue exclusive to substance abuse problems[9]. Once again, this is the reason for the application of an interdisciplinary methodology to address the problem of drug addiction: it provides an opportunity to look at the conjunction of the neurobiological sphere with the sociopolitical sphere in order to better understand a phenomenon that by its very nature arises out of a miscommunication between these two different disciplines that try to understand human behaviour; it provides an opportunity to see how an area of study of the underlying brain functions related to intention and motivation can be so disconnected from the policies aiming to regulate that very same human behaviour.

Notes

1 The sense here being that addiction may be thought of as a brain disease, and if we are to adhere to that explanatory model of addiction, then understanding a psychoactive substance's action on the brain is crucial to an understanding of what makes the substance "addictive". Other viewpoints may very well place the locus of the "addictive" quality of substance consumption elsewhere.

2 An example of this in the United States is the Mental Health Parity and Addiction Equity Act (MHPAEA), enacted in 2008, which requires health insurers as well as group health plans to guarantee the same financial support structures for mental health and/or substance abuse as for medical and surgical requirements. https://www.govinfo.gov/content/pkg/PLAW-110publ343.pdf/PLAW-110publ343.pdf.

3 "Deaths related to drug poisoning in England and Wales: 2020 registrations". Deaths related to drug poisoning in England and Wales from 1993 to 2020, by cause of death, sex, age, and substances involved in the death. https://www.ons.gov.uk/peoplepopulationandcommunity/birthsdeathsandmarriages/deaths/bulletins/deathsrelatedtodrugpoisoninginenglandandwales/latest.

4 "Trends and Developments report presenting the latest analysis of the drug situation in Europe. Focusing on illicit drug use, related harms and drug supply, the report contains a comprehensive set of national data across these themes and key harm reduction interventions". https://www.emcdda.europa.eu/publications/edr/trends-developments/2021_en.

5 Release and Harm Reduction International's response to DHSC's Naloxone Consultation (2021, September 30). Release. https://www.release.org.uk/publications/release-and-harm-reduction-international%E2%80%99s-response-department-health-and-social-care.

6 "The Global State of Harm Reduction" provides an independent analysis of harm reduction in the world. It is a comprehensive global mapping of harm reduction responses to drug use, HIV, and viral hepatitis. https://www.hri.global/global-state-of-harm-reduction-2020.

7 "The INCB Annual Report, prepared in accordance with the three international drug control treaties, examines the global drug control situation and makes recommendations to Governments and regional and international organizations". https://www.incb.org/incb/en/news/AR2021/incb-2021-annual-report-and-precursors-report-launched.html.

8 "The 1961 and 1971 Conventions classify controlled substances in four lists or Schedules, according to their perceived therapeutic value and potential risk of abuse. Included in an annex to the 1988 Convention are two tables listing precursor chemicals, reagents and solvents which are frequently used in the illicit manufacture of narcotic drugs and psychotropic substances. This treaty also significantly reinforced the obligation of countries to establish criminal offences in order to combat all aspects of the illicit production, possession and trafficking of psychoactive substances". https://www.tni.org/en/publication/the-un-drug-control-conventions#:~:text=There%20are%20three%20United%20Nations,Traffic%20in%20Narcotic%20Drugs%20and.

9 If one considers the existing arguments for sugar and high-calorie food consumption to be an addiction of a certain kind, this could be a similar case to the one I describe with substance abuse. For the sake of my argument, I will make a distinction based on the fact that these policies have the avowed intention of reducing a certain problem related to the consumption of sugar and high-calorie foods, whereas substance abuse problems are exacerbated when a policy is aimed at treating it in such a way that is conceptually different from what the problem actually is (i.e., criminal behaviour instead of a medical disorder).

References

Barnett, A., Hall, W., Fry, C.L., Dilkes-Frayne, E., & Carter, A. (2018). Implications of Treatment Providers' Varying Conceptions of the Disease Model of Addiction: A Response. *Drug and Alcohol Review*, *37*(6), 729–730. https://doi.org/10.1111/dar.12844

Buchman, D.Z., Skinner, W., & Illes, J. (2010). Negotiating the Relationship Between Addiction, Ethics, and Brain Science. *AJOB Neuroscience*, *1*(1), 36–45.

Clark, T. (2021). Determinism and Destigmatization: Mitigating Blame for Addiction. *Neuroethics*, 14. https://doi.org/10.1007/s12152-020-09440-w

Costa, A.M. (2007). *Free Drugs or Drug Free? Speech at the Drug Policy Alliance Conference*, New Orleans. Available at: http://www.unodc.org/unodc/en/frontpage/free-drugs-or-drugs-free.html

Evans, C.J., & Cahill, C.M. (2016). Neurobiology of Opioid Dependence in Creating Addiction Vulnerability. *F1000Research*, *5*, F1000 Faculty Rev-1748. https://doi.org/10.12688/f1000research.8369.1

Hall, W., Carter, A., & Forlini, C. (2015). The Brain Disease Model of Addiction: Is It Supported by the Evidence and Has it Delivered on its Promises?. *The Lancet Psychiatry*, *2*(1), 105–110. https://doi.org/10.1016/S2215-0366(14)00126-6

Heather, N., Best, D., Kawalek, A., Field, M., Lewis, M., Rotgers, F., Wiers, R.W., & Heim, D. (2018). Challenging the Brain Disease Model of Addiction: European Launch of The Addiction Theory Network. *Addiction Research & Theory*, *26*(4), 249–255. https://doi.org/10.1080/16066359.2017.1399659

Holton, R., & Berridge, K. (2013). Addiction Between Compulsion and Choice. In N. Levy (Ed.), *Addiction and Self-Control* (pp. 239–268). Oxford University Press. https://doi.org/10.1093/acprof:oso/9780199862580.003.00122

Leshner, A.I. (1997). Addiction Is a Brain Disease, and It Matters. *Science*, *278*(5335), 45–47. https://doi.org/10.1126/science.278.5335.45

Maté, G. (2012). Addiction: Childhood Trauma, Stress and the Biology of Addiction. *Journal of Restorative Medicine*, *1*(1), 56–63. https://doi.org/10.14200/jrm.2012.1.1005

Morse, S. (2003). *Diminished Rationality, Diminished Responsibility*. Faculty ScholarshipatPenn Law. 525.

Morse, S. (2013). A Good Enough Reason: Addiction, Agency and Criminal Responsibility. *Faculty Scholarship at Penn Law*. https://scholarship.law.upenn.edu/faculty_scholarship/1605

Pickard, H. (2017). Responsibility Without Blame for Addiction. *Neuroethics*, 1–12.

Pickard, H., & Ahmed, S.H. (2016). How do you Know you Have a Drug Problem? The Role of Knowledge of Negative Consequences in Explaining Drug Choice in Humans and Rats. *Addiction and Choice: Rethinking the Relationship*, 29–48.

Pickard, H., & Ahmed, S.H. (Eds.). (2019). *The Routledge Handbook of Philosophy and Science of Addiction*. Routledge.

Poland, J., & Graham, G. (Eds.). (2011). *Addiction and Responsibility*. MIT Press.

Ross, D., Kincaid, H., Collins, P., & Spurrett, D. (Eds.). (2010). *What is Addiction?* MIT Press.

Seddon, T. (2009). *A History of Drugs: Drugs and Freedom in the Liberal Age*. Routledge.

Trujols, J. (2015). The Brain Disease Model of Addiction: Challenging or reinforcing Stigma? *The Lancet Psychiatry*, *2*(4), 292. https://doi.org/10.1016/S2215-0366(15)00050-4

Volkow, N.D. (2001). Drug Abuse and Mental Illness: Progress in Understanding Comorbidity. *American Journal of Psychiatry*, *158*(8), 1181–1183. https://doi.org/10.1176/appi.ajp.158.8.1181

Volkow, N.D., Koob, G.F., & McLellan, A.T. (2016). Neurobiologic Advances from the Brain Disease Model of Addiction. *New England Journal of Medicine*, *374*(4), 363–371. https://doi.org/10.1056/NEJMra1511480

Volkow, N.D., Poznyak, V., Saxena, S., & Gerra, G. (2017). Drug Use Disorders: Impact of a Public Health Rather than a Criminal Justice Approach. *World Psychiatry*, *16*(2), 213–214. https://doi.org/10.1002/wps.20428

Wiss, D.A., Avena, N., & Rada, P. (2018). Sugar Addiction: From Evolution to Revolution. *Frontiers in Psychiatry*, *9*, 545. https://doi.org/10.3389/fpsyt.2018.00545

Chapter 2

A Philosophical View

Agency and Action in the Context of Addictive Behaviour

Introduction

There is an apparent paradox in addictive behaviour: why do addicted persons continue to engage in a behaviour and/or consume a substance which they are aware is detrimental to their health and wellbeing? The philosophical concept at the core of this question is that of agency. More specifically, the idea that addicted persons might lack agency or at least exhibit signs of "diminished" or otherwise "compromised" agency. Neuroscientific research into addiction focuses on the compromised agential capacities exhibited by addicted persons, and this concern over agency underlies our moral attitudes towards addicted persons: "Why do they make the wrong choice?" This type of research also focuses on our moral attitudes concerning the responsibility and burden of blame for the actions of addicted persons, which underlies a concern into the nature and aetiology of addiction as a disorder: "If it isn't a choice, what makes them compelled to act as if it were?" Finally, neuroscientific research hones in on the problem that policy measures often have to grapple with, i.e. the tension between respecting the freedom of choice of individuals and the need to deal with their compromised decision-making processes regarding their addictive behaviour, a concern that underlies the political debates surrounding addiction as a social phenomenon requiring policy solutions: "How best do we deal with and/or treat people making such detrimental choices, regardless of whether or not it is they who make them?"

Agency is therefore central to the question of addiction, regardless of the disciplinary perspective through which we analyze it, and in this chapter, my purpose will be to develop a theoretical framework for the understanding of a particular kind of agency in the context of addiction, in order to better incorporate such a concept into the strategies of harm reduction aimed at dealing with addiction in political debates. In discussing the ontology of what an addicted action is, I will draw on the standard concept and theory of action, as it has developed in analytic philosophy within the second half of the 20th century.

DOI: 10.4324/9781003582908-3

Rationalization as a Sufficient Causal Explanation for Actions

Though I will place my arguments for the contextualization of addictive behaviour within a framework of action theory, I will not provide an exhaustive review of every branch of the philosophy of action. Rather, I will draw upon the authors and theories which I believe can provide the basis for the development of my preliminary question "How should we understand agency and action in the context of addictive behaviour?"

"*The philosophical career of Donald Davidson started with action theory, and modern action theory more or less started with Davidson*". Ralf Stoecker (2010)

In 1963, Davidson published "Actions, reasons and causes" (ARC), into a field which had hitherto been largely influenced by a Wittgensteinian school of thought that denied a positivist relationship between language and thoughts/actions. In other words, the causes for our actions could not be found in what we expressed about them. Davidson's work went against this idea and defended a causal theory of both action and its consequent explanations. Davidson characterized actions as a type of event whose causal explanation lay in the explanation communicated by the agent, i.e. its rationalization, and in so doing laid the foundation for what would become a standard concept in the philosophy of mind and action, the "belief-desire" model of motivation.

With the context for Donald Davidson's theory of action in mind, we can see the relation between linguistic descriptions of action and their place in an ontology of action, i.e. how propositional logic can be the foundation for first-order logic in an attempt to codify language surrounding action. For Davidson, the nature of an event must be discernible from various descriptions of said event. Though *moving his arm up and down* and *replenishing the house's water supply* is technically a valid description of the action of a man filling a cistern with water, they are different descriptions of the same event and need further context to be said to be describing the action of that man (Anscombe, 1957). For Davidson, *flipping a light switch* and *alerting a burglar who happens to be in the house* are also different valid descriptions of the same event, but crucially not the same action due to the inherently distinct intentionality and post-hoc rationalization for said event.

Two central ideas are at the heart of the Davidsonian account of agency. The first concerns the "primary reason" for an action, which Davidson describes as a 'pro-attitude' towards a goal (i.e., to have a positive desire to attain something) paired with the belief that a certain action will bring about that goal (e.g., I flip the switch because I want to turn on the light and I have every reason to believe that my flipping the switch will result in the light being turned on). An action is then explained by its context within a rational pattern of behaviour, and the desire-belief pair is central to a Davidsonian account of agency.

In Donald Davidson's account of an action's cause, the rationalization by the agent provides the reason and thus cause for an action (Davidson, 1963). The view that Davidson defends is that an explanation of an action by reference to reasons, and in subsequent formulations the "intention" of the agent, is indeed the causal explanation for said action, by virtue of the fact that those stated reasons *explain* the action (e.g., I moved my arm *because* I wanted to reach for my pen). This type of explanation is labelled a "rationalization" by Davidson and served as an opposition to explanations that relied on the causality of physical laws of nature (e.g., the pen falls to the ground *because* of the force exerted on it by gravity). Rationalizations fit into a larger pattern of behaviour and were thus distinct from explanations that relied on law-like causes.

It is important here to establish a clear understanding of what Davidson means when he speaks of "rational", and by extension the sense in which we have to understand that term when operating that concept. We can commonly refer to an action as "irrational" when its efficiency in achieving a supposed goal is put into question, thereby implying the essential feature of "rationality" to be the logical mechanical solution to any given problem or situation. It is "irrational" for me not to take an umbrella with me if it's raining (assuming that all other things considered I do not wish to get wet). However, there is an implied morality in the usage of the term "rational", when we qualify the value of actions, and there is a sense in which a Davidsonian account of agency could prove problematic for the context of addiction, if it relies on the "rationale" behind an action that furthers a consumption or behaviour deemed addictive. In the case of addicted actions, there is a common sense in which they are labelled "irrational". Taking the example of nicotine and tobacco, it is commonly said that smoking cigarettes is an "irrational" action, at least in our current context, if we assume the person smoking has all the relevant information regarding the health risks associated with nicotine and tobacco. Knowing how dangerous and detrimental to one's health smoking cigarettes can be, it is "irrational" to continue smoking. Here again, we are confronted with the paradox of addiction that was mentioned earlier: Why would a person make a choice that is detrimental to their wellbeing?

There is an implied value judgement in that statement, and before we delve into an ethical analysis of addiction and the consideration and treatment of addicted persons, we have to establish a distinction between the moral connotation of that statement and the use of "rationalization" by Davidson's account of an action's causality. Davidson does not imply a value judgement, nor moral character to the action being "rationalized". In Davidson's sense, it is an explanation rather than a justification of the action. In such an understanding of the term "rationalization", we can indeed apply it to addicted actions without the value judgement attached. If we adhere to the normative value of health and wellbeing as worth pursuing, an addicted person does not make "rational" choices in consuming a substance that is detrimental to both, yet it is entirely possible to "explain the motivation" of their addicted actions, through a Davidsonian "rationalization" of the underlying mechanics of their addiction (i.e., the neural, psychological, environmental, and emotional reasons for the actions which led to their consumption of an addictive substance and subsequent continuation of consumption of said substance).

This brings us to an interesting question regarding the possibility of "rationalizing" addictive behaviour. How should we understand the "rationalization" of addicted persons for their actions, in a Davidsonian sense? Does their first-person account seem compromised? If so, what makes their "rationalization" capacity different from that of any other "irrational" action "rationalized" by an agent (e.g., I didn't take my umbrella with me, even though it was raining, because I felt the urge to recreate the famous scene from *Singin' In The Rain* on my way to work)? In this sense, there is a variety of scales, and on a small enough view we can understand the logic behind each action leading up to addiction, thus "rationalizing" it, even though it continues to be an "irrational" action. This can take the form of every seemingly innocuous action, conscious or otherwise, leading a person towards further consumption of their substance of choice, finally reaching oft-connotated rationalizations like "Just one more won't hurt".

The second idea of Davidsonian accounts of agency is that an action is explained by being described in a particular sense, and its content changes once that description changes. In other words, the ontology of an action, in a Davidsonian view, is dependent upon the prism through which it is described and thus carries a heavily subjective facet. I have already alluded to the example Davidson uses, of a light switch being flipped in a house being burglarized unbeknownst to the person flipping said light switch: that same event can equally be described as *alerting the burglar*. One event can be described in different ways (e.g., I flip the switch, I illuminate the room, I alert the burglar, etc.). An event is then distinct from an action in Davidson's description, where the same event may refer to different actions, subjectively. This second idea, once again applied to the specific case of an addicted action, will prove slightly more troublesome to conciliate. We can understand an "addicted action" by describing a seemingly innocuous event, unrelated to the actual consumption of an addictive substance, yet be seen as an "addicted action" nonetheless (e.g., driving down the street... towards the liquor store to buy alcohol). Through this larger scope, we can potentially reconcile Davidson's second idea with the case of "addicted actions".

Davidson's argument is laid thus:

1. For us to understand how a reason of any kind rationalizes an action, it is necessary and sufficient that we see, at least in essential outline, how to construct a primary reason.
2. The primary reason for an action is its cause.

(*Actions, Reasons, and Causes*, 1963)

The link that Davidson attempts to establish is that the "primary reason" for an action (the desire-belief pair) is not only an explanation of the action, it is also causal, inasmuch as it causes the action to happen. This is why the rationalization of an action can serve, according to Davidson, as a causal explanation of it as well, and thus as the basis for the genuine locus of agency. The distinction of Davidson's account, and what separates it not only from its contemporary opposing views on mechanistic explanations of behaviour but also subsequent attempts at conciliating stated reasons with law-like explanations, is the refusal to adhere to predictive possibilities of this account, denying the notion that a rationalization could be reduced to a non-rational explanation of action such as the mechanistic one necessary for any scientific method aiming to predict action and behaviour from pre-existing conditions such as predispositions of behaviour. This Davidsonian framework serves as an early precursor to our current debates on the nature of free will and neurobiological determinism, but we will keep such discussions for a later segment[1].

The nuance one could anticipate within this account, for the context of addiction, would be the formation of beliefs, and how those might be disrupted by the chemistry of the brain when in contact with an addictive substance, as well as the formation of desires and the malformation of which could be due to abnormal surges of dopamine in the brain (Hyman et al., 2006), once again due to exposure to addictive substances. One first implication of a Davidsonian account we must address then is the predilection for rationality as a standard justification for any kind of action, at the cost of what would have to be considered "irrational" behaviour in the case of actions not borne out of stated desires. Indeed, the idea that addicted behaviour is irrational certainly has its proponents but is not the same conceptually as would be the opposite of a "rationalization" account of addictive behaviour according to Davidson's view of agency.

The question we are left with is then the following: how ought we to consider the validity of self-stated rationalizations for addictive behaviour by addicted persons? Standard theories of belief-formation and desire-seeking as causal explanations for actions would have to accommodate the malformation of them by addiction, and therefore lead to a "compromised" level of agency, if we were to stick with a Davidsonian account. A further question we would have to address would then be what kind of agency would count as "uncompromised" and if there is any sense in considering a type of agency informed by beliefs or desires borne out of disrupted neural circuitry as "genuine".

Addictive Behaviour in the Context of Action Theory

Davidson's work established a major part of the debate surrounding the analytic conception of an action's intentionality as explained by desires, beliefs, and mental states in general. Indeed, as we have alluded to previously, one of the central debates around the philosophy of action in the 20th century is the causality attributed to agency from actions that are perceived as intentional, i.e. we attribute a sense of agency to a subject forming intentions and subsequently being able to execute those intentional actions. Conceiving of an action in terms of its intentionality is in some form an ascription of causality to said intention. According to the standard theory of action that emerges from Davidson's work, there is a close connection between an intentional action and the notion of having acted for a reason. The ontology of an action and the discussion of what constitutes it from the standpoint of the agent is relevant for our discussion of the context of addiction, and brings us to a specific question: How can we describe "addicted actions" in a Davidsonian manner?

In the context of addiction, we must clearly establish an ontological distinction between an action and an addicted action. If we are to consider addiction as a distinct phenomenon, it stands to reason its manifestation through the addicted agent has to be distinguished from the non-addicted agent. In later discussions, we might be able to shift the point of distinction from the agent's external manifestations towards the agent's internal state of mind, their physical brain, even their neural circuitry, and such distinctions might very well have consequences for our moral attitudes towards it and our measures applied to it, but before all that, we have to clearly categorize what we understand to be an action and an *addicted* action.

By an addicted action, I will understand an action, here in the standard Davidsonian conception of an action, as formed by an intention that directly or indirectly brings about a manifestation of an agent's addiction. For example, if the agent in question is addicted to alcohol, a direct action might be the taking of a sip of an alcoholic beverage, thus ingesting the drug of choice and very explicitly engaging in their addiction. However, though not a direct action, that same agent going to a liquor store to purchase alcohol or going to a pub/bar in order to consume alcohol will equally be considered an addicted action. Indeed, from an isolated view, the act of putting on one's coat, taking one's keys, getting into one's car, or stepping out of the house and walking towards a certain place might not be considered to be part of an addiction, yet they all form part of a causal chain of events that lead to the direct action of consuming the drug in question and thus engaging in the addiction. In Davidsonian terms, the event is the same, while the action is described differently, and could thus subjectively be a different action.

In order to conciliate the distinction between descriptions, the intention of any of the previous actions is goal-oriented towards the moment of consumption. The agent gets into their car, turns the key, and begins to drive in the direction of the store with a clear intention and knowledge of those actions being links in the chain of events that will lead to more consumption of alcohol. This distinction is important because on the surface many other actions might be similar and from an external point of view might be indistinguishable, and described differently. A person walking along the street and happening upon a liquor store, seeing the liquor store, and feeling a triggering sense of craving for alcohol and thus stepping inside to buy alcohol has to be ontologically different, from an agential point of view, than a person deciding to walk to the liquor store with the intent of buying alcohol. In almost every way the two actions are the same. Both persons are walking, engaging the exact same mechanical function of their legs to propel them towards the liquor store, but the intention of the agent is not the same, and thus through post-facto rationalization would be distinct. Therefore, at least from a Davidsonian account, making them different actions. Though the relation with responsibility, and more specifically moral responsibility, will have its place in a later part of this book, it is crucial to allude to its place in the distinction of the intentionality of an action here. In one case, it can be said that a person was simply walking down the street, and upon seeing the liquor store, they fell victim to their addiction. The proximity to the store, the sudden realization of the distinct and real possibility of consuming alcohol, and the surprise and unintended nature of the event of seeing the liquor store are all cues that trigger the memory and knowledge (embedded on a deep psychological and neurobiological level within the person's mind and brain) and thus compel (more on this notion later) the person to walk inside the liquor store, and purchase and consume alcohol.

Many caveats can be made here. Did the person not remember that there was a liquor store on this particular street? Was this an unconscious ambulation towards an oft-frequented place, were their feet dragging them, unbeknownst to them, towards the very place they unconsciously really wanted to go? Questions about the nature of unconscious actions and their explanation, as well as the moral discussion over dessert and blame for unconscious actions, deserve their own development and are beyond the scope of this chapter. For now, what is important is the distinction within the context of conscious actions, between the different goals that drive an action or sequence of actions.

In keeping with the previous context of Davidson's rationalization theory, we can understand an addicted action as one made and rationalized with the intent of engaging in an addiction or to further the goal of engaging in an addiction. In the case of the person happening upon the liquor store, the action of walking down the street is not an addicted action. As soon as the liquor store comes into their view and they decide to go in, every action that brings about their consumption of alcohol is now an addicted action. Distinctly, in the case of the person who leaves their house *to go* to the liquor store, the same action of walking down the street is an addicted action. To summarize, any action is an addicted action if:

- The action directly engages the agent with their addiction (e.g., drinking an alcoholic beverage).

or

- The action indirectly brings about the intentional goal of the agent of directly engaging with their addiction (e.g., intentionally walking towards the liquor store).

A crucial point of contention within addiction studies is not in the distinction of an addicted action from a non-addicted action, but rather how said addicted action might come to be considered to be part of the addiction itself. Indeed few people would consider walking down the street to be a morally reprehensible action, a manifestation of a disrupted neural circuitry, or even a psychological exhibition of compulsive behaviour. Yet, in the context of addiction, as we have previously seen, that action is a causal link in a chain of events very clearly directed towards the goal of engaging with an addiction (consuming alcohol). Moreover, in the context of a Davidsonian account of agency, that very same action, for example "walking down the street", might very well be described differently, for example "looking for a fix". In many self-reported accounts, addicted persons will describe in detail the feeling of compulsion and lack of self-control in a variety of tiny, isolated actions, which might not seem indicative of an addiction (e.g., frequenting a known place for drug dealing, walking in the direction of a liquor store, etc.), but which nonetheless form part of an entire pattern of behaviour directed towards the ultimate goal of procuring an addictive substance for consumption (Heyman, 2009). The nuance in which our discussion must focus is then the formation of that goal and the way in which a conscious decision to engage with an addiction can be formed. Following Davidson's distinction between an action and *acting for a reason*, our distinction between walking down the street and *walking down the street towards the liquor store in order to buy and consume alcohol* serves as an example of the distinction that should be made between an action and an addicted action.

The purpose of contextualizing action within a state of addiction is ultimately the more ethical treatment of addicted persons. In order to treat addicted persons better, we need to legislate them better. In order to legislate them better, we need to understand their neurobiological condition better. In order to understand their neurobiological condition better, we need to understand the norm of what an action is better, thus understanding what an addicted action is in that context. In order to do that, we needed to review a standard theory of action and apply addiction to that context, which is precisely the objective of this chapter. A further consideration in the following chapters, and something for which we can establish the foundation now, are the ethical implications for that conception of addiction in a theory of action.

The Place of Responsibility in the Context of Addictive Behaviour

Following on from Davidson, many authors then focused on the question of responsibility in the context of an intentional action, and what would count as an intention and a fair attribution of responsibility. Here the nuance would lie in the paradox often stated by addicted persons: their self-stated intention NOT to consume and yet their consumption nonetheless, for example "I have no desire to act on my addictive craving, but I do so anyway". In describing his view on the concept of responsibility, John Martin Fischer distinguishes between *causal responsibility*, *role-responsibility*, and *moral responsibility* (Fischer, 2010). Herein, the addicted person is perhaps causally responsible for their own actions, though whether it falls upon them to be attributed the moral responsibility is in question.

> One is causally responsible for some upshot insofar as one is part of the causal chain leading to that upshot, quite apart from whether one is morally accountable for it (or morally accountable at all). So, for example, the lightning bolt might be causally responsible for the fire, the earthquake for the crack in the roof, and an individual who sneezed loudly might be causally responsible for waking up the baby. [...] There might also be cases in which an agent is morally but not causally responsible for an upshot, but this is a bit more contentious. Imagine, for example, that one does not initiate or contribute 'positively' to a causal sequence issuing in a certain upshot, but that it is one's duty to prevent the upshot, and one intentionally fails to prevent it. This is arguably a case of moral responsibility for the upshot without causal responsibility, although it might be argued that one has caused the upshot through one's omission to act.
>
> (Fischer, 2010, p. 309)

The consequence of an attribution of agency to a subject is then the moral responsibility to which they must be held for actions stemming from their own agential capabilities. In later discussions, the compromised nature of said agential capabilities will be crucial in distinguishing from responsibility and culpability (legal or otherwise), but for now we can limit ourselves to the abstract notion that being morally responsible simply means *"being accessible to or an appropriate target for certain distinctively normative responses"* (Fischer, 2010).

In fleshing out the notion of moral responsibility in a context of addicted persons, and especially in a context of a bioethical discussion of addiction, we must inevitably contend with the overlap that can occur between schools of thought on both the concepts of *responsibility* and *autonomy*. Harry Frankfurt developed a hierarchical analysis of the notion of "acting freely" in the context of moral responsibility. Frankfurt uses the language of "first-order" and "second-order" preferences (wherein the "second-order" preferences are a metatextual preference over what the first-order preferences are, i.e. not what one *wants* but what one *wants to want*). Frankfurt additionally creates a subset of categories in "second-order" preferences, where "second-order" volitions are preferences over which preferences we wish to move us to act on said preferences (Frankfurt, 1971). Frankfurt uses the notion of a hierarchical approach to provide what he considers to be a "free action", i.e. an action that can be said to originate from one's free will, if there is harmony between the first-order preferences and second-order volitions.

In this context, we can then understand how addictive behaviour represents an excellent case study in free will and the application of Frankfurt's hierarchical theory of agency in the context of first- and second-order preferences: an addicted person will undoubtedly have a first-order preference for the consumption of whatever substance he is addicted to. However, it will more than likely be the case that upon reflection, they will state second-order volitions that are not in sync with those, i.e. they recognize wanting to consume the substance but wish they didn't want to. In other words, and according to many witness accounts of people in the throes of an addiction (Heyman, 2009), they do not consider themselves to be acting of their own free will when consuming the addictive substance, even though mechanistically in the moment they do have a first-order preference to consume rather than not.

The essence of Frankfurt's theory can be found in other current permutations, such as "dual-system" or "dual-process" regarding decision-making. In this view, two distinct types of mental processes are at the root of our deliberative internal decision-making and thus manifest agency in the following way: the first system (System 1) is typically considered as fast, automatic, largely instinctive, and nigh effortless to execute, while the other (System 2) is considered slow, deliberative, and based on rules. While some form of dual-process theory can be applied to most areas of research into psychology and behaviour, those most relevant to our need for a theoretical background of agency in addictive behaviour concern the philosophy of mind and cognitive science, with perhaps some relevant discussion of behavioural economics (Kahneman, 2011).

In this context, and following from the Davidsonian framework of rational agency we have operated in so far, there is an assumption regarding the use of one sole mechanism of reasoning that is at the root of agency. Indeed the "rationalization" in Davidson's account does not seem to be *prima facie* compatible with a dual-system approach to understanding compromised agency, but it could serve as useful in an understanding of the paradox of the self-stated rationalizations of what are commonly seen as "irrational" actions on the part of addicted persons. One difficulty in understanding dual-processes stems from the lack of consensus on how the two systems interact with one another. One common assumption is that there is a top-down hierarchy of System 2 being the one in control and having the capacity to override System 1, while an inverse chronological order of System 1 being the first responder to any given situation, with System 2 intervening only when necessary (the difficulty in establishing that point is evident in most of the literature: exactly when and how does System 2 intervene? And why does it intervene on certain occasions and not on others?). Interaction and interference between the two systems would seem to be the perfect framework for a case study involving addicted actions and has indeed been explored in some instances (Simon & Daw, 2012). This is not entirely different from the first-order/second-order distinction in Frankfurt's hierarchical analysis of free agency. If indeed System 2 is considered as hierarchically superior, i.e. overlooking System 1, then it is simply a different manner of describing Frankfurt's view on freedom of will as the result of synchronization between both systems (orders of preference).

Upon first view, indeed it seems incompatible to apply a dual-system theory to a Davidsonian account of self-stated 'rationalization' for an addicted action, because it is implied that the 'rationalization' would fall under the purview of System 2 exclusively. Yet, if we were to make some semantic adjustment to the conceptualization of what 'rationalizing' entails exactly in Davidson's sense, then we could potentially apply a dual-system approach to understanding not only agency and action itself, but even the *post hoc* rationalization of an addicted action.

This consideration of compatibility between a dual-system theory and the specific context of agency theory has indeed been the subject of interest (Schlosser, 2019) and provides a starting point for further exploration. Tentatively the two approaches of a Davidsonian "rationalization" of addicted actions and the problem of compulsivity could be conciliated on the basis of intentionality as the point of contention between a System 2 *post hoc* "rationalization" of a disrupted System 1 automatic response to craving triggers in the context of addiction. In this sense, when the neural disruption caused by an addictive substance manifests itself, it would only be System 1 that is compromised by addiction, where System 2 would remain intact and would indeed be the part of the agent still "in control" and responsible for both the feelings of regret and negative reactions to one's own behaviour (clarifying the apparent paradox of addictive behaviour to which I've alluded previously), and subsequently for the incentive to override the addictive impulses and resist addictive cravings, whether successfully or not. The disruption of the (System 1/System 2) communication is what could theoretically be at the root of paradoxical addictive behaviour. This novel theory, though semantically distinct, might simply help in the visualization of agential disruption in an addiction context. The broader question that will interest me for the moment is whether or not it is helpful in explaining addictive behaviour in a constructive and ethically sound way for further use in neurobiological explanations and/or policy measures.

The Free Will Debate in the Context of Addictive Behaviour

So far, I have tried to demonstrate how the application of a Davidsonian account of action theory to the context of addictive behaviour in general can prove challenging. But this is even more apparent when faced with the traditional debate of what free will is and how it affects our notions of moral responsibility, autonomy, and the nature of self-control. If we were to apply the case study of addiction to the various philosophical positions around the free will debate, we would see how different perspectives influence our perception of agency in addiction.

Determinism

Determinism is the position that states that all events, including human actions, are determined by prior causes, following the laws of nature. If determinism is true, then every action, thought, and decision made by us is the inevitable result of the state of affairs in the universe and the universal laws of physics. In the context of addiction, this raises a troubling question: if a person's addictive behaviour is determined by factors beyond their control – such as genetics, brain chemistry, or even environmental influences – ought they be held responsible for their actions?

Some philosophers have addressed this dilemma by examining the nature of moral responsibility in a deterministic framework (Fischer & Ravizza, 1998). They argue that moral responsibility does not require absolute free will but rather a certain kind of control over one's actions, which they label "guidance control". This control involves the capacity to respond to reasons and to guide one's behaviour in accordance with those reasons, even if the underlying causal mechanisms are determined.

In the case of addiction, a determinist would argue that an addicted person's condition is entirely predictable and inevitable given the initial conditions of their birth (genetics, environment, culture, etc.) and thus would absolve them completely from a moral standpoint. On the other hand, Fischer and Ravizza might argue that while the initial development of addictive behaviour may be influenced by factors outside a person's control, the individual still retains some degree of "guidance control". For example, they may recognize the negative consequences of their addiction and make efforts to seek treatment or avoid triggers. From this perspective, an addicted person could still be held morally responsible for their actions, even if their ability to exercise free will is severely limited by their addiction.

Compatibilism

Compatibilism offers a middle ground in the debate, arguing that free will and determinism are not mutually exclusive. According to compatibilists, individuals can be considered free and morally responsible as long as they act in accordance with their desires, intentions, and rational deliberations, even if these are causally determined.

Fischer and Ravizza's theory of moral responsibility is often seen as a form of compatibilism. They contend that what matters for moral responsibility is not the absence of causal determinism but the presence of certain internal states, such as the ability to recognize reasons and to control one's actions in light of those reasons. This view has important implications for the context of addiction.

For example, an addicted person might be seen as morally responsible for their actions if they retain the capacity to recognize the harmful effects of their addiction and to take steps to mitigate those effects. Even if their addiction is the result of deterministic factors, such as genetic predisposition or environmental components, they can still be held accountable for their choices, provided they have the ability to act on their reasons.

However, even in a compatibilist framework, we must also acknowledge that addiction can impair an individual's capacity for rational deliberation and self-control. In severe cases, where addiction overwhelms a person's ability to respond to reasons, a compatibilist might argue that the individual is less morally responsible, though not entirely absolved of responsibility. This nuanced approach allows for a more compassionate understanding of addiction, recognizing the complex interplay between determinism and agency.

Libertarianism

Libertarianism, in contrast to determinism and compatibilism, asserts that free will is incompatible with determinism. Libertarians argue that for individuals to be truly free and morally responsible, we must consider their actions entirely undetermined by prior causes. Instead, individuals must have the capacity to make genuinely free choices, unbound by deterministic constraints.

In the context of addiction, libertarianism presents a more challenging view of moral responsibility. If addictive behaviour is determined by factors beyond an individual's control, then that individual cannot be held morally responsible for their actions. However, libertarians might argue that even in the face of addiction, individuals retain the capacity for free choice, even if in a limited form.

For instance, a libertarian might claim that while addiction exerts a strong influence on behaviour, it does not completely eliminate the individual's ability to make free choices. An addicted person might still be able to choose to seek help, resist temptation, or adopt healthier habits, even if those choices are difficult. From this perspective, the moral responsibility of the addicted person is maintained because the individual retains the capacity for free will, despite the challenges posed by addiction.

The philosophical debate on free will offers valuable insights into our understanding of agency in the context of addiction. Determinism, compatibilism, and libertarianism each provide different perspectives on the nature of free will and moral responsibility, shaping how we view the actions of individuals struggling with addiction. While determinism and compatibilism emphasize the role of internal states and rational deliberation in moral responsibility, libertarianism highlights the importance of genuine free choice. It is important to keep all of these perspectives in mind, for they contribute to a more nuanced and compassionate understanding of addiction, acknowledging both the constraints and possibilities inherent in human agency, something which will be crucial in our discussion of how the public ought to consider and ultimately govern addicted persons.

Conclusion

> Our moral responsibility for action depends on the fact that we ourselves determine the way we act. The question, then, is what kind of self-determining power we really exercise. For that will provide the true basis of our moral responsibility. Is it that we are exercising a power to act otherwise? Or is it that we are acting as we will, and because we so will? Which matters – control or voluntariness? The idea of freedom as two-way voluntariness is an attempt to combine both conceptions. But it is a deeply unstable compromise, and control is surely going to be the loser. And this is because, on this theory, the power to act otherwise is never actually being exercised to determine action – only a power to act as one wills. Why make moral responsibility depend on it, if it is irrelevant to any power that the agent actually exercises over the way he acts?
>
> (Thomas Pink, 2010, p. 307)

Our notion of being morally responsible for our actions stems from the intuitive notion that we are free to determine the way we act, hence the necessary passage through a philosophical discussion over agency and free will in the discussion of the moral responsibility of addictive actions. Far from the notion of addicted persons' moral responsibility being tied to the resolution of the free will/determinism debate, it does raise the issue of what remaining, if any, power of volition an addicted person possesses, and how such power may be measured. Such questions, the nature of the exercise of volition, and the hijacking of that faculty through the action of addictive substances on our neurocircuitry will be the subject and focus of the next chapter, precisely in order to help the discussion over the basis of addicted persons' moral responsibility over their actions, from a more empirical standpoint. Is it neurobiologically possible for an addicted person to have acted otherwise with regard to their craving, wanting, and ultimately seeking of the substance in question? What measure of self-control is left in them?

I have explored here the theoretical framework for the conception of addicted actions as the Davidsonian view on "rationalization" as causality for action, and the formation of intention as crucial in an ontological distinction between action and *addicted* action. I have reviewed some of the problems such accounts encounter when faced with the concept of compulsion and its ubiquity in the context of addictive behaviour, as well as other normative challenges to the standard conception of agency stemming from Davidson, which could prove problematic for the context of addicted actions. Finally, I have cited some current dual-system theories that could potentially bridge that divide and provide a conciliatory means of resolving the addictive behaviour paradox within a Davidsonian theoretical framework for agency.

This is but a preliminary exploration of what a theoretical framework for the conception of agency in the context of addiction might look like. One in which we understand an addicted action as one made and rationalized with the intent of engaging in an addiction or to further the goal of engaging in an addiction, and which provides an understanding of the paradox of the self-stated rationalizations of what are commonly seen as "irrational" actions on the part of addicted persons, thus bridging the divide between a dual-system approach to understanding addicted persons stated goals and desires, and a Davidsonian standard "belief-desire" model of action.

Many questions still remain, and crucially the ethical dimension of what this conception entails remains to be discussed and assessed for the purposes of further application in policy measures. As I mentioned at the beginning, though the argument of this book will be constructed from multiple disciplinary perspectives, it was important to begin with a foundational discussion on the philosophical concepts of agency, action, intentionality and compulsion, as well as touching on some key aspects of what those concepts mean for moral responsibility, and the other different kinds of responsibility that might be construed with respects to addictive behaviour.

The final destination on this road is a discussion of the public health policy strategies that are put in place to deal with some of the issues affecting addicted persons, but before getting there, it will be necessary to make a pit-stop at the paradigmatic shift that has occurred in neuroscience and its conception of addiction as a brain disease. The debate between the "brain disease" model of addiction and the "moral choice" model of addiction has been widely discussed and I will not pretend to provide a novel angle in either camp. Rather, my objective in the following chapter will be to provide an overview of the neuroscientific research into addiction and show how it mobilizes concepts such as free will and compulsive behaviour. I will try to steer the discussion clear from the binary debate over the nature of addiction as either a brain disease or a moral choice, all while avoiding the trappings of a neuroreductionist view of addiction.

Note

1 Indeed, Davidson's account of rationalization as cause for action is relevant in current camps of rebuttal against deterministic accounts of an addicted person's predisposition to consume. Within that theoretical framework, indications of neurobiological mechanisms for addiction would be understood as manifestations of the agent's rationalization of their behaviour but would not indicate a possibility of predictive power from said observations.

References

Anscombe, G.E.M. (1957). *Intention*. Oxford: Blackwell.

Davidson, D. (1963). Actions, Reasons, and Causes. *The Journal of Philosophy*, *60*(23), 685–700. https://doi.org/10.2307/2023177

Fischer, John M. (2010). Responsibility and Autonomy. In *A Companion to the Philosophy of Action* (pp. 309–316). John Wiley & Sons, Ltd.

Fischer, J.M., & Ravizza, M. (1998). *Responsibility and Control: A Theory of Moral Responsibility*. Cambridge University Press.

Frankfurt, H.G. (1971). Freedom of the Will and the Concept of a Person. *The Journal of Philosophy*, *68*(1), 5. https://doi.org/10.2307/2024717

Heyman, G.M. (2009). *Addiction: A Disorder of Choice*. Cambridge, MA: Harvard University Press.

Hyman, S.E., Malenka, R.C., & Nestler, E.J. (2006). Neural Mechanisms of Addiction: The Role of Reward-Related Learning and Memory. *Annual Review of Neuroscience*, *29*(1), 565–598. https://doi.org/10.1146/annurev.neuro.29.051605.11300999

Kahneman, D. (2011). *Thinking, Fast and Slow*. New York: Farrar, Straus and Giroux.

Pink, T. (2010). Free Will and Determinism. In *A Companion to the Philosophy of Action* (pp. 301–308). John Wiley & Sons, Ltd.

Schlosser, M.E. (2019). Dual-System Theory and the Role of Consciousness in Intentional Action. In B. Feltz, M. Missal & A. Sims (Eds.), *Free Will Causality and Neuroscience*. Brill Editions.

Simon, D.A., & Daw, N.D. (2012). Dual-system Learning Models and Drugs of Abuse. In *Computational Neuroscience of Drug Addiction* (pp. 145–161). New York, NY: Springer.

Stoecker, R. (2010). Davidson. In T. O'Connor & C. Sandis (Eds.), *A Companion to the Philosophy of Action* (pp. 58–65). Wiley-Blackwell.

Chapter 3

A Neuroscientific Perspective

The Brain Disease Model of Addiction and Reductionism

1 Background for the Brain Disease Model of Addiction

Having established a philosophical framework of action theory from which we can study addictive behaviour, I now turn to a neuroscientific perspective of that phenomenon. To be specific, this chapter will serve as a brief summary of how the neuroscientific perspective on addiction came to be shaped, and specifically how it coalesced into the now widely accepted paradigm of addiction as a brain disease, commonly referred to in the literature as the National Institute on Drug Abuse (NIDA) brain disease view. After a brief overlook of the neurobiology of addiction and particularly of the view of addictive behaviour understood as a consequence of the "hijacking" of a person's neurocircuitry, I will discuss how this empirical knowledge came to be used in the construction of such a wide-reaching and influencing paradigm as the NIDA brain disease view, which has affected so many different areas of our societal and political attitudes towards addiction.

In this discussion, I will explore the relationship between a neuroscientific consensus and policy construction and see whether there is a feedback loop that can occur when the establishment of such a paradigm becomes politically and socially useful, which can then compromise the epistemological value of the scientific model. This will be of particular interest in the final chapters of my book concerning the ethical analysis of the different legislatures that have been used to deal with addicted persons. The objective of this chapter, and its importance within the broader scope of my book, is to look at the history of how the brain disease paradigm came to be shaped, first by specific scientific advances and discoveries, and then by sociopolitical evolutions in discourse, in order to then assess the effects of the wider acceptance of this brain disease model to the point of becoming a paradigmatic shift in the broader area of addiction studies. My hope is to shed light on the ethical implications that a neurocentric view can have on the political attitude towards a human behavioural problem, how it can alter the course of a societal phenomenon being observed and as such shape the data being used to construct the policies aimed at resolving it. In so doing, I hope to lay the

DOI: 10.4324/9781003582908-4

groundwork for the main concern of this book, i.e. policy constructs that adopt or reject this neurocentric view and incorporate it (or not) into their evidence-based approach to public health policy construction.

A Brief Summary of the Neuroscience of Addiction

Addiction, from a medical diagnostic standpoint, is a relapsing disorder characterized by compulsive drug taking having negative effects on the subject's life, accompanied by a dependence on said drugs as manifested by withdrawal syndromes occurring upon attempts at cessation. From a neurobiological perspective, several neural processes are affected during the development of this disorder. These processes are affected both by the chemical composition of the drug and the very act of seeking and taking the drug over time as well. Indeed, there is a clinical distinction between the occasional use of a substance and the continuous and repeated use of said substance, which is then considered an addiction. The ongoing objective of neuroscientific research is to understand the mechanisms by which recreational use can tip over into compulsive drug-taking which is characteristic and necessary for the clinical diagnosis of an addiction. Compulsive drug-taking requires the following three major elements:

1 compulsion to seek out the drug;
2 loss of control in limiting the intake of the drug;
3 the emergence of a negative emotional state if access to the drug is prevented.

In this section, I will attempt to provide a brief overview of the neuroscientific study of drug addiction. My intention is to present the context within which the underlying neurobiological mechanisms of addiction, and what we have come to understand about them, are contrasted with the psychological, social, and environmental aspects of addiction. This contrast is meant to serve as a backdrop to the further discussion that I will undertake regarding the political ramifications of our understanding of addiction, as well as the legal frameworks that we ought to put in place to better address this public health issue. An exhaustive review of the entire neuroscientific field of research on addiction is beyond the scope of this chapter, but in providing this brief overview I do hope to succinctly summarize the general tenets of our current understanding of the underlying neural mechanisms that characterize addiction as a chronic and relapsing disorder that arises from an initial recreational drug use to compulsive and continuous drug taking.

Moreover, as the following overview will show, neurobiological research into the function and effect of addictive substances on the brain is not conducted in a conceptual vacuum, and both clinical and behavioural social science research are intertwined along the lines of research that neuroscientists embark upon in order to better understand the vulnerability of individuals to succumb to an addiction as a result of an interaction between their genetic makeup, environmental cues, and biopsychosocial frameworks of understanding behaviour. These interactions can be examined through the lens of a neuroscientific study of the effects of addiction in the brain, which manifest themselves as biochemical and functional aspects of different types of neurotransmitters and circuits.

Specifically, the consensus from the neuroscientific research into addiction over the last few decades has favoured a view in which certain addictive drugs "hijack" the neurocircuits usually involved in the modulation of emotion and motivation, which then results in the impaired decision-making process of the individual and their apparent "loss of control" over their actions, namely the taking or not taking of the drug. These alterations are the result of chronic consumption of the drug in question and create deep-seated memories that trigger cravings and thus lead to the relapsing aspect of addiction.

It is important to note that in constructing a comprehensive understanding of addiction, one level of analysis cannot encompass the entire phenomenon that is addiction, and as such even within the already-restricted disciplinary perspective that is neuroscience, the development of what we conceive of as the disorder of addiction will involve various levels of analysis: the chemical properties of the substances involved, the neural circuits on which they have an effect, the individual's genetic predisposition to certain substances and their effects, their life experience, the presence of psychological disorders that may trigger consumption, comorbidity with related mental disorders, and others. This is without mentioning, of course, the broader conjunction of these factors with environmental cues, sociocultural factors, and the general context in which the drugs are being consumed. A comprehensive understanding of addiction must incorporate empirical knowledge on how the brain functions, but should also take into account the individual's entire surroundings, both spatial and temporal, as well as their sociocultural background, and how these will have a deep influence on how the individual's brain will operate, and thus what their behaviour will be. The purpose of this chapter is then twofold within the structure of my book: first, to provide a complementary neuroscientific basis for the previous discussion on addiction as a kind of manifestation of "compromised agency"; and second, to provide the context for the recent debates in UK legislature concerning the diagnosis of addiction as a medical affliction, which will be the basis for my discussion on the ethical implications of policies regulating addicted persons.

How Reward is Coded in the Brain

One of the main lines of animal research that led to our current neuroscientific understanding that all addictive drugs have a commonality in the way they affect the brain was a series of experiments conducted in the 1950s, which involved the stimulation of specific brain regions in rats (Olds & Milner, 1954). This led to the discovery of certain regions in the brain that were associated with feelings of "pleasure" and "reward", by observing how the rats continuously sought out the stimulation of these areas, even going so far as ignoring food and water in order to continue to receive that stimulation. These areas of the brain came to be known as the "pleasure center" of the brain, and later on as "brain reward regions" (Schultz, 1998).

Subsequent research, and more detailed observation of these areas, allowed neuroscientists to find the more specific pathways that mediate this type of stimulation (Wise, 1978). One such pathway is the ventral tegmental area (VTA), located within the midbrain region, which connects with a structure called the nucleus accumbens (NAc). The nucleus accumbens serves as the mediator between several brain structures of the limbic system, which is the system commonly associated with the control of emotions, and the striatum, which is the system commonly associated with the initiation and control of bodily movement. The nerve cells in the brain, what we refer to as neurons, communicate with each other through neurotransmitters, chemical substances that relay signals from one cell to another via synapses, structures that permit the passage of electrical signals. Dopamine is one of the primary neurotransmitters used by the brain reward circuits and features heavily in the neurobiological study of addiction since it functions as a reward signal in the brain circuitry and is present in the four main classes of drugs featured in substance addiction research, i.e. nicotine, alcohol, stimulants, and opioids (Koob & Volkow, 2010).

This broad schematic of the interaction between neurons of the VTA and the nucleus accumbens serves to illustrate how dopamine fulfils the function of communicating between different regions of the nervous system, and thus how any perturbation in the balance of this chemical substance may have consequences in the regions it traverses (Cooper et al., 1996). The chemical neurotransmitter will be located in the transmitting nerve cell and will be released once the nerve cell is stimulated. The neurotransmitter will then pass through the synapse and bind to a receptor (specific sites that recognize the chemical makeup of the neurotransmitter) in the receiving nerve cell. This receiving neuron will then either be excited, inhibited, or be altered chemically in some other way.

Another major line of research into the underlying neurobiological mechanisms of addiction stemmed from this insight into the reward pathways of the brain: highly addictive drugs seem to activate, or behave like, the neurotransmitters involved in the brain reward circuitry (Robbins et al., 2007). Opioids, for example, behave like endorphins, endogenous chemical compounds in the brain (neuropeptides and/or peptide hormones) that are produced and stored in the pituitary gland and are secreted to relieve stress and pain. Cocaine and other similar stimulants enhance dopamine release, while nicotine behaves like acetylcholine, which is a neurotransmitter that sends signals to contract muscles, dilate blood vessels, and slow the heart rate down. Alcohol enhances the activation of gamma-aminobutyric acid (GABA), a major and ubiquitous neurotransmitter in the brain which functions as a natural inhibitor of receptor nerve cells (Di Chiara and Imperato, 1988). These are but a few examples of the ways in which some addictive substances mimic the functions of naturally occurring neurotransmitters in the brain. This summary is by no means exhaustive and each neurotransmitter can serve many other functions at different levels of the brain. Yet it is important to note how the discovery of this mimicking trait at the chemical level is at the root of how addictive substances affect brain function. Furthermore, these examples all show how the common factor among all drugs is the regulation of the brain rewards circuits that connect the VTA and the nucleus accumbens, one of the major breakthroughs throughout the recent decades of neuroscience research into the effect of addictive substances in the brain (Berridge & Robinson, 1998).

It is equally important to note that each drug will affect many different neurotransmitters and can have secondary functions. The effect of a certain chemical substance in the brain will not be restricted to one neurotransmitter in one area; they can excite neurons within a variety of intracellular levels, and produce chemical and molecular changes that can affect gene expression, which would then translate into tertiary indirect effects of the drug (Koob, 1996). For example, reuptake mechanisms are the reabsorption of the neurotransmitter into the presynaptic neuron through transporting channels. This is necessary for normal synaptic function because it permits the recycling of neurotransmitters and regulates the number of neurotransmitters present in the synapse, controlling the strength of the signal. Cocaine will inhibit the reuptake mechanism of serotonin, a key chemical substance associated with mood and wellbeing, and norepinephrine, a stress hormone and neurotransmitter that serves to increase heart rate, blood pressure, and sugar levels in order to provide more energy. By inhibiting the reuptake mechanism of these chemicals, cocaine has the effect of increasing their natural actions within the synapse and thus their receptors. These secondary functions of addictive drugs will equally contribute to the alteration of dopamine pathways, the previously mentioned major neurotransmitter connecting the VTA and the nucleus accumbens. Research conducted with dopamine neurons showed that when they are affected, destroyed, or inhibited, significant brain function alterations in reward pathways were observed. Any alteration to the action of dopamine will equally affect the balance among other neurotransmitters in these areas of the brain (Berridge, 2004).

The Effects of Drugs on Reward Pathways

The type of effect that a drug will have on the brain depends on its chemical composition and function (e.g., both cocaine and opioids reinforce dopamine synaptic presence, but due to their different chemical function, opioids are sedating while cocaine is a stimulant). The common site of action for all addictive substances is the brain reward pathway (O'Brien, 1996). However, a drug's action will be determined by the neuroreceptors for that drug and where they are located in the brain, which can many times be located outside of that reward pathway. Under normal and unaltered brain function, dopamine is released and subsequently inhibited by the reuptake mechanism that takes the neurotransmitter back to its presynaptic nerve cell (Koob, 1992a). Having consumed cocaine, a person's reuptake mechanism of serotonin and dopamine is blocked, leading to a buildup of dopamine in the synapse (Pierce & Kumaresan, 2006).

Having consumed amphetamines, on the other hand, reverses the reuptake mechanism, causing the presynaptic neuron to release more dopamine than usual. Both cocaine and amphetamine have the same effect of enhancing the stimulation of dopamine pathways that lead to the "brain reward centers" by essentially having more dopamine present in the synapse, but they come to this result through different neurobiological alterations (Hyman, 1996).

Opioids, on the other hand, can alter neurocircuits in different ways, depending on the chemical composition of the substance in question. The limbic system, a set of brain structures that deals with emotion and memory, consists of neurons with opioid receptors, especially in the nucleus accumbens, which allows for opioids to act upon these brain regions directly (Berke & Hyman, 2000).

Synthetic opioids, like morphine, have a similar structure to endogenous opioids, like enkephalins, and can cause the nerve cells in the VTA to release more dopamine by binding with natural inhibitory neurons and thus stopping their action, resulting in a destabilized rate of dopamine being released. This augmented release of dopamine results in a stronger stimulation of the brain reward centres and an imbalance between dopamine and other neurotransmitters (Hyman et al., 2006).

Alcohol and nicotine also have a disinhibitory effect on neurons in the VTA, causing an enhanced dopamine release in the same neurocircuits. Ethanol will increase the release of dopamine neurons and result in higher dopamine levels in the nucleus accumbens, exerting its action on various sites in these regions which modulate dopaminergic activity both in the VTA and the nucleus accumbens. Ethanol is also involved in the negative reinforcement of dopaminergic activity, such as relief of withdrawal symptoms (Koob & Le Moal, 2008).

What this neurobiological model provides in relation to the study of addiction is first and foremost an empirical statement of the clear and observable effects on brain function that psychoactive substances have.

It equally shows the cascading effect of long-term drug use, and the difficulty in promoting cessation of use by sheer will of the addicted person as the most viable treatment option. Hence, this neurobiological model promotes a de-stigmatization of drug addiction. Later on in this chapter, I will focus more on the debating views of addiction as a moral disorder or a brain disease, and the use of neuroscientific views to destigmatize and de-politicize addicted persons. This model shows how agency can be said to be compromised, albeit in a heavily neuroreductionist view of how brain neurocircuitry can affect decision-making. This will be of interest in later chapters, where the notion of a liability and criminal responsibility defense may call upon a neurobiological view of addictive behaviour. Finally, and of most importance to the central question of this book, a look at the neurobiological model of addiction provides a solid basis for arguments geared towards medical harm reduction as a more ethical method of treatment and recovery for addicted persons.

The Role of Memory in the Transition from Recreational Use to Compulsive Addiction

The clinical diagnosis of addiction as a disorder, as has been stated in the neuroscientific literature, relies on a variety of general principles, one of which is the observable aspect of recreational use leading to compulsive consumption of addictive substances (APA, 2013). Having focused on the reward pathways that are affected by the consumption of an addictive drug, we can now take a look at the neurocircuits that are involved in the process of emotions, adaptive learning, and behavioural conditioning whose changes translate into this passage from recreation to compulsive use. Such neurocircuits will categorize objects in the world (e.g., pleasurable, desirable, dangerous, repulsive, etc.) and subsequently modulate circuits in the brain that are responsible for the reaction to those objects (e.g., approach, ingest, avoid, etc.). The connections between the circuits that regulate these emotional responses to objects in the world and the circuits that encode memories are the underlying mechanisms for what we understand as memories with strong emotions associated with them (Koob, 1996). Think of a toddler burning their finger or smelling a delicious meal. Such encoded memories will influence subsequent behaviour when reintroduced to the same sensory cues. This is of course an oversimplification of a hugely complex neurobiological mechanism, but it serves to introduce the neurobiological aspect of the role of encoded memory in addiction that I will focus on here.

The previously mentioned reward pathway connecting the VTA and the nucleus accumbens, through which dopamine is transmitted, is thought to have evolved in order to regulate behaviour that was required for survival and reproductive success, such as sexual attraction and food consumption. Memories of a rewarding experience are likely to be vivid, carrying with them positive emotional layers. Therefore, this reward neurocircuit more than likely plays a similar evolutionary adaptive role in assigning specific behavioural responses to any type of new stimulus that triggers similar reward cues. This is the general basis for the neuroreductionist explanation for drug addiction: the emotional overtones associated with the stimuli of a novel drug being consumed will make the brain more vulnerable to said drug because it mimics the neurotransmitters that are associated with the natural evolutionary responses of that cue. In a way, addictive drugs are tapping into a very strong emotional shortcut in the brain that signals a positive evolutionary response.

Here a small caveat may be worth mentioning. Although the location of the neuroreceptors will influence the effect that a substance will have on the brain, it is important to note that other properties also determine a drug's effect. The quantity of a drug in the brain, as well as the rate of increase in that level, will play a large part in its effect. This is why, for example, the mode of consumption of a drug will have an influence on its effect on the brain (Kalivas & Volkow, 2005). If a drug is smoked or injected, it will have a different effect than if it is ingested orally. This is due to the speed with which the substance will reach the brain when it is consumed this way. This is not to say that speed of consumption completely overrides total quantity (i.e., alcohol consumed in large amounts, even though consumed orally, will still have a profound impact on the brain), but it does help explain why the same drug administered in different forms will result in differing levels of addiction (e.g., "crack cocaine" being smoked and exposed to the lungs' larger surface area will be far more addictive than powdered cocaine being consumed nasally, which in turn will be far more addictive than chewed coca leaves)[1] (Wilkinson et al., 1980).

Long-term Changes in Brain Neurocircuitry

One of the key points of the neuroscientific literature, and now-widely accepted paradigm of addiction as a brain disease, is that continuous and frequent consumption of a certain drug for a sufficiently long period of time will result in changes in the brain (Leshner, 1997). These changes will be the result of homeostatic responses that compensate and adapt to the excessive presence of a chemical component in the brain. These changes are what can in some sense be pointed to as the physically observable aspect of addiction, and they can be categorized into three different types:

1 Opioids and alcohol will result in adaptations in brain regions that regulate somatic function and will produce physical dependence. This is mainly why the sudden removal of those substances can lead to physically observable withdrawal symptoms, such as hypertension, irregular heartbeat, tremors, and different types of seizures (Di Chiara, 2000).
2 All addictive drugs produce adaptations in the brain reward pathways described earlier. Some of these adaptations will contribute to high tolerance levels to the substance, thus contributing to the increased dosages

required for the drug to have the same effect on the individual, thus resulting in an escalating cycle of even more acute addiction to the substance and ever higher dosages, etc. This will equally result in affective withdrawal symptoms when the drug is suddenly removed (e.g., depression, drug cravings, etc.).[2]

3 Strong emotional memories associated with drug use can be another concrete, though difficult to observe, brain change stemming from long-term drug abuse (Beck et al., 1992). The dopaminergic circuitry triggered by addictive drugs has a direct effect on the strength of the memories that are associated with drug consumption. This is one of the neurobiological brain changes that therapists and clinicians will point to when speaking of the importance of crave-triggering cues and why they must be avoided by a person attempting to stave off relapse (Newman, 2001). These cues are the memories associated with the drug use and can induce a strong craving upon the mere thought of them. These memories, which cue the relapse, are associated with the risk of relapse and have been the subject of a lot of research and have yielded some results in the concept of cognitive-behavioural psychotherapy as a method of treatment for drug addiction (Luborsky et al., 1995; Marlatt and Donovan, 2005).These changes in brain structure are by no means uniform and vary wildly depending on the individual and drug in question. Somatic withdrawal symptoms may last days or weeks, and the memories associated with the strong emotions felt while consuming the drug may never quite leave a person's psyche (Heyman, 2009).

These observable changes in the physical structure of the brain are linked to the immaterial notion of memory and emotion, and it is that link between grey matter and emotion that is at the heart of one of the biggest conceptual leaps that the neurobiology of drug addiction has been able to establish: the initially freely-made choice of engaging in consumption of a drug will result in a lived experience that will have a physical impact on their brain and may lead to physical dependence on that drug and thus a compulsive (and arguably less free) choice to continue consuming.

A Neuroscientific Perspective on Vulnerability to Addiction

From a neurobiological standpoint, it is quite possible to identify the physical reasons why an individual might become vulnerable to compulsive desires to continue consuming a drug that will negatively impact their wellbeing once the initial consumption has taken place (Kreek et al., 2005). However, this is not the only reason or factor in an individual's vulnerability to addiction, and indeed a multiplicity of other reasons might exist. A neuroscientific perspective is simply one way of categorizing addiction as a clinically observable disease of the brain.

The general manner in which recreational use can lead to compulsive consumption has been broadly described, and the same type of research has detailed certain risk factors for a brain succumbing to that physical dependence (Cloninger et al., 1988). These factors will lead to increased consumption, while others will increase the likelihood that however much or little the individual consumes the drug, it will have a strong and captivating effect on their brain. These factors can be both genetic as well as environmental and will influence the willingness of an individual to partake of a certain drug and their subsequent risk of developing dependence.

Little is known about the genetic predispositions to cocaine, opioids, or tobacco addictions, while a lot more research has discovered clear genetic components of vulnerability to alcohol addiction. Studies that have looked at identical twins separated by different adopting families have shown that early onset alcoholism can be linked to genetic predisposition regardless of environment, while later life onset alcoholism seems less so and much more influenced by environmental factors (Rhee et al., 2003).

Studies that have looked at adverse reactions to alcohol among certain ethnicities would suggest a factor of genetic predisposition to intolerance to alcohol, biologically founded on the variation of certain genes that code for two major enzymes responsible for alcohol metabolism, alcohol dehydrogenase (ADH), and aldehyde dehydrogenase (ALDH2), which are located within the mitochondria of the cell (Thomasson et al., 1991; Thomasson et al., 1994). A deficiency in ALDH2 caused by a genetic variation has been found to be an inheritable trait, leading certain individuals to be completely intolerant to alcohol. A deficiency in ADH has a lesser effect of alcohol aversion in the individual but is comparable and can equally lead to reduced tolerance.

These studies show the link between certain genetic variations and alcohol tolerance. Animal modelling has been used among species that show similar reactions to alcohol as humans, mostly in studies looking at tolerance levels and reaction to pharmacological interventions, such as naltrexone, in order to stimy the effects of alcohol in the system. This type of research has the objective of finding pharmacological options for treatment, and they are based on the foundation of genetic predispositions to alcohol (Li & McBride, 1995; Johnson, 2005). Gene mapping techniques have been used in order to identify a variety of genes with sections associated with alcohol preference, sensitivity, tolerance, and withdrawal (Nestler & Aghajanian, 1997). In the next section, I will focus more specifically on whether a neuroreductionist approach can be of any benefit in the conceptualization of addiction, looking in particular to notions of destigmatization and the mitigation of blame in cultural views of an addicted person's responsibility for their behaviour. For now, it is worthwhile to take note of the myriad of avenues possible in the neurobiological field of addiction studies, if only to demonstrate the different levels at which evidence can be presented etiologically and how the case can be made for a conceptualization of addiction that is medicalized and based on neurobiologically observable changes in a person's brain circuitry.

What this type of research can tell us is that the brain can have multiple points of vulnerability through which addictive behaviour can be manifested. This can be a valuable addition to our understanding of human decision-making systems, especially within theories of the brain as a complex network of interacting systems (planning, habitual behaviour, situation recognition, etc.). Indeed, a neurobiological map of the brain's reaction to continuous exposure to psychoactive chemicals has helped researchers identify key vulnerabilities in the human decision-making system, such as euphorigenic "reward-like" signals, as detailed previously, and overvaluation in the planning system of the human mind, which can account for the incentive salience of drug cravings (Redish et al., 2008).

This is why it is important to find a place for genetic research within the broader field of addiction study and even neuroscientific study specifically. Research on certain genes may be associated with higher levels of risk of addiction, and research into the variations that translate to increased vulnerability represent promising avenues for future treatment options (Reich et al., 1998). A greater focus on this type of research can also help in more accurately situating it within the multiple behavioural, biopsychosocial, and environmental factors that come into play in the study of addiction and provide a complete and more holistic strategy for treatment options that involve all these different disciplinary approaches (Buchman et al., 2010). The availability of drugs, and the social and cultural environment in which the individual finds themselves, all contribute to a person's vulnerability to fall into addictive behaviour, and the observable neurobiological changes in the brain offer a glimpse into the physical manifestation of this disease. Once again, this is a point that will be further developed in the following chapter, but it remains important to contextualize this broad field of neuroscientific research on addiction with the social and political evolution of the narratives that have shaped the problematization of addiction. The nexus of harm reduction strategies that have come to the forefront of public discourse on addiction recently find their evidentiary justification, as well as their normative argumentation bolstered, by the sheer preponderance of neuroscience research that shows how addiction can very well be conceptualized as a disease that affects the circuitry of the brain associated with emotional and volitional control.

The Social and Policy Context of the NIDA Brain Disease Paradigm

Over the years, this body of work from the field of neuroscience of addiction has given rise to the "NIDA paradigm", which can be used as a shorthand for the consensus view within the neuroscientific literature that addiction can be best understood as a chronic and relapsing brain disease, a consequence of long-term drug-taking which results in the loss of control that characterizes most addicted persons' habitual drug consumption. It is an established view that was most prominently championed in the late 1990s by the director of the National Institute for Drug Abuse at the time, Alan Leshner (Leshner, 1997), and which continues to be widely supported in the neuroscientific literature today (Volkow et al., 2016).

This view was not immediately accepted, and to this day continues to be challenged by alternate perspectives on the study of addiction (Heyman, 2009) and scepticism over the ability of neuroimaging techniques to explain complex behavioural phenomena such as addiction through deterministic bottom-up explanations of damaged neurocircuitry (Satel & Lilienfeld, 2013). While resistance to a new scientific paradigm is not a historically new phenomenon, it is worth noting that the political, social, and sometimes clinical opposition to this particular paradigm was unusual (Courtwright, 2010). What would normally appear as a major scientific breakthrough seems to have been met with scepticism and an unwillingness to adopt what the neuroscientific community regarded as uncontroversial: that the neurocircuitry of the brain is disrupted as a result of continuous and persistent drug consumption, and that this disruption then leads to observable loss of control and compromised decision-making processes on the part of addicted persons.

Some attempts have been made to clarify the controversial nature of this paradigm (Volkow & Koob, 2015), and the inclusion of a social context, a genetic component, and comorbidity with other mental and behavioural disorders into the standard understanding of the paradigm has been slow but steady over the years. Yet the basic tenets of the brain disease view have remained quite unchanged in the past few decades since its introduction into the literature: persistent and continuous use of addictive substances leads to long-term changes in the brain structure and function.

How the paradigmatic view of addiction as a disease came into being is just as important as current sociopolitical trends and tensions when it comes to deciphering the nature of addiction and our social response to it. Through improved instrumentation and more advanced laboratory technology, the NIDA paradigm of addiction as a brain disease was made possible through financial efforts made to support research into the field. Certain examples of advances that made this paradigmatic view possible are: intracranial self-stimulation in rats, the observation of the endogenous opioid release system in human beings, the mapping of certain neuro-receptors and their function, a better understanding of substance sensitization and dendritic morphology, the mapping of the mesolimbic dopamine reward pathway, and finally the discovery of single-nucleotide polymorphisms (variations in DNA sequences) that predispose a risk for addiction (Koob et al., 1998). By themselves, not one of these discoveries or advances in neuroscience would be enough to establish a completely different understanding of addiction, but taken as a whole they paint a convincing picture that addiction should be considered a brain disease because it is an observable behavioural disorder that can be causally traced to pathological changes in the neurocircuitry of the brain (Koob & Simon, 2009).

The brain disease view has bolstered, and at times encumbered, four main groups of people who deal with addiction as a major component of their job: medical personnel, who treat addicted persons as patients; police and law enforcement agencies, who deal with the correlated crimes and social harms associated with addiction; social scientists, who study addiction through the lens of its social construction and an emergent property of social behaviour in vulnerable populations; and finally politicians and policymakers, who ultimately determine the laws and regulations that control the legal (and consequently the illegal) access to drugs, not to mention the penalization and different treatment responses to addicted persons convicted of the previously mentioned correlated crimes.

This last point will be developed a lot further in subsequent chapters, but here it is worthwhile pointing out that the agencies which were tasked with reducing the prevalence of addiction and related problems like overdoses and crime all but copied the NIDA's language to describe addiction to certain substances and thus justify their efforts. For example, according to the Drug Enforcement Agency (DEA) of the United States, long-term abuse of certain substances could lead to "a chronic, relapsing disease, characterized by compulsive drug-seeking and drug use which is accompanied by functional and molecular changes in the brain" (DEA, 2009). There is of course a broader context involving geopolitical motivations to slow down the supply of illicit drugs from foreign countries, but the general argument was difficult to refute: if the NIDA's brain disease paradigm was indeed correct, then drug exposure in a population could lead to a lot of suffering and social harms, thus justifying the general strategy of harsh prosecution and reduction of the supply.

Where the argument should have led to a less conservative outcome, at least in theory, was in the criminal justice system, where the individual's control over their addiction could be put into question. Harsh punishment would seem inappropriate if the NIDA's brain disease view was accepted by the judicial system. It could be argued that our current criminal justice system's response to the brain disease view seems paradoxical and/or unethical. Indeed, the brain disease view is accepted by governments and agencies when they are using it to accentuate the risk and danger of letting the illicit substance flow into the population; while when it comes to the individual, the legal system seems to ignore the same discourse, not accepting the same argument that would absolve a person of their actions due to the observable and demonstrable compromised decision-making process (Redish et al., 2008).

As a means of legal defense, a paradigm that puts into question the individual's ability to exert self-control is crucial, and the debate around the issue remains to this day. Once again, this is but an allusion to a much more complex issue which will be dealt with in subsequent chapters, but for now it is worth noticing the many areas in which the neuroscientific paradigm of addiction as a brain disease had an effect. In a much broader sense, it is only one perspective through which we can attempt to understand a particular aspect of human behaviour (i.e., loss of self-control) in a very specific set of circumstances (i.e., due to long-term exposure to psychoactive substances), and what the consequences of this new understanding ought to be in terms of policy and regulation of said human behaviour. The philosophical implications of the NIDA brain-disease view of addiction for our folk notions of intention, and the ethical implications for our methods of policy construction, will be discussed in further detail in the following chapter.

Summary

Neuroscientific research on addiction has greatly evolved over the past few decades. The location of specific brain regions involved in emotion, memory, and decision-making has been crucial to understanding the link between consuming a substance and the effects on behaviour in an individual. Neuroreceptors and the transmitters involved in reward pathways have been studied and continue to intrigue researchers as to their exact functioning upon alteration by addictive drugs. The importance of the dopaminergic circuitry has been thoroughly established as one of the major sites of action for addictive drugs. And the correlations between certain substances and the blocking of reuptake mechanisms in synaptic function have been a great example of the physically observable phenomenon of a neuroreceptor binding site that directly contributes to the abuse of a drug (Koob, 1992b).

The summary I have described in this section is but a very brief recapitulation of decades of research into the neuroscience of addiction and is what has led to the widely accepted paradigm of categorizing addiction as a brain disease. Generally speaking, this model describes addiction as a disease of the nervous system, in which brain changes stemming from continuous consumption of the drug lead to an inability to control one's urges and drug-seeking behaviour.

Equally important has been the development of treatment options stemming from this research, which is aided by the identification of common pathways of reward stimulation and the brain structures involved in its regulation. I have already mentioned some examples of medication directly stemming from this type of research (e.g., naltrexone as an opioid function antagonist) (Volpicelli et al., 1992; O'Malley et al., 1996).

Other than to help develop pharmacological treatment options, the scientific curiosity that motivates research into addiction is the confounding aspect of it: the notion that a chemical component may lead inexorably once consumed to the "hijacking" of the motivational and behavioural neurocircuits of an individual's brain. Addicted persons will indeed exhibit behaviour that seems somewhat paradoxical from a behavioural point of view. This stems from the basic contradiction of continuing a behaviour that is known to them to be detrimental to their health and wellbeing, not to mention the social and personal cost that it may take on their lives. While this may seem paradoxical from a behavioural level, we have seen that this can be perfectly explicable from the neurobiological level of analysis. Hence the importance that must be given to this view and modelization of addiction in establishing preventative measures, be they social, personal, or pharmacological, underlining the fact that the most important method of combatting addiction is preventing that initial jump from recreational use to compulsive consumption.

The comorbidity of addiction with a host of other mental disorders is an important aspect to note in both the concern over vulnerability and treatment for the disorder. Psychotic disorders can alter dopaminergic function, for example, and thus present higher levels of risk when the individual is susceptible to drug abuse. The opioid epidemic in the United States and other parts of the world also highlights the great risk that some medications may present to patients taking medication for a number of other illnesses (Dowell et al., 2016). The interaction between the individual, their neurobiological and genetic makeup, and their sociocultural environment, all contribute to the risk of addiction. Understanding the inherently complex and interdisciplinary approach needed to fully grasp the problem of addiction is necessary in order to provide an equally comprehensive solution to that problem.

This broader context is important not only for a comprehensive understanding of the phenomenon but also because it serves to dispel the notion that addiction and its associated moral component are a binary concept: addiction is a result of either wilful choice or an inherent genetic determinant. The broader context for the onset of addiction and its development in the brain serves to mitigate and nuance the conception of addictive behaviour. Much like other genetic predispositions to certain diseases (coronary conditions, diabetes, etc.), the clinical diagnosis of risk factors may involve genetic variation, often confounded with family history, and yet leave open the possibility of avoiding the disease if the choice is made by the patient to follow doctors' advice and take proper preventative medication, for example.

The field of neuroscientific research on addiction continues to attract a lot of interest, and even more so as more and more is discovered regarding the complexity of this phenomenon from a neurobiological standpoint. Many questions remain regarding the way in which drugs can alter brain structures and thus influence behaviour, through control of decision-making processes and emotions. The importance of continuous research into the physical manifestation of addiction in the brain is unsurprisingly linked to the objective of developing medication and pharmacological intervention methods for addiction treatment. Some advances have been made in this area, such as naltrexone or methadone, both used as an opioid detoxification medicine, yet no "miracle pill" to cure addiction has yet been developed, nor is likely to ever come. The common notion in addiction treatment is that a strong social and emotional support system is key in helping the individual slowly recover and undo the long-standing brain structural changes brought on by addiction.

II Against Neuroreductionism

An in-depth look at the neuroscientific research into addiction, and an understanding of the recent emergence of the NIDA brain disease view, might give the impression that the paradigmatic shift of conceiving of addiction as a medical disorder is a relatively new phenomenon. However, the general concept of addiction as a disease had begun to take shape at the beginning of the 19th century in both the United States and the United Kingdom (Levine, 1978), even though said conception involved a more archaic view of alcoholism as a progressive disease (intemperance) that ought to be treated through total abstinence. In a way, the epistemological debate over the medicalization of this condition began over a century ago, it continues to this day (Heyman, 2009), and it has been re-ignited with arguments coming from the neuroscientific field which aim to provide conclusive proof that addiction truly is an observable, physical, neurobiological condition (Leshner, 1997; Volkow & Fowler, 2000). The philosophical counterargument from certain authors is that a demonstration of *any* action as being truly compulsive is nigh impossible (Levy, 2010), and that the best neuroscience can do is provide a merely descriptive account of the neural circuitry involved when addictive behaviour occurs (Stephens & Graham, 2009). Compulsion, of course, being a key tenet in the modelization of addiction as a disease. If saying that a person suffers from an addictive disorder means that they literally cannot resist the impulse to consume the substance in question, then the view of addiction as a "brain disease" has a much stronger foundation.

The objective of this section will be to untangle some of the debate between the neuroscientific perspective on the underlying mechanisms of addictive behaviour and the philosophical understanding of the causal theory of action in the special context of addiction. As this discussion will show, neuroscientific research necessarily mobilizes concepts such as free will, compulsive behaviour, and the nature of a disease, all of which can benefit greatly from a philosophical grounding. Meanwhile, a philosophical inquiry into the nature of action and addictive behaviour equally benefits from a solid understanding of the data and empirical knowledge provided by neuroscientific advances. This conversation between the two perspectives will serve to lay the foundation for the upcoming discussion on public health policy and the ethical implications for the treatment of addicted persons.

I can situate this interdisciplinary dialogue here, having already spent some time discussing the neuroscientific perspective that posits that addiction is best understood as a disease. Here, I will focus on its relationship with the concepts I unpacked in the first chapter dedicated to the philosophical account of addictive actions, namely the distinction between intentionality and involuntary action, and the notion of a compulsive and non-autonomous action. Indeed, if we can agree that addiction represents a compulsive mode of action, then the argument for its treatment as a disease has a much stronger footing, which is precisely the angle through which some have argued against the disease view (Fingarette, 1988).

Secondly, having already spent some time in the first chapter going over the elemental notions of action and intentionality, I will not give an exhaustive account of the free will debate here. Instead, I will examine specific points of confusion regarding the nature of a "free human action" that can arise in certain areas of neuroscientific literature. This will help provide some context for the ongoing debate among philosophers and neuroscientists around the epistemological basis for the classification of addiction as a disease, which will then provide the necessary background for the construction of evidence-based public health policies aiming to treat addiction in a more clinical manner, rather than a criminal one. The most famous of these points of confusion regarding the nature of a "free human action", and by far the most contentious, have been the Libet experiments (Libet et al., 1983), which claimed to demonstrate that human action was not under conscious control. The ensuing arguments against free will have already been largely problematized (O'Connor, 2005; Mele, 2006), and here I will simply argue that the entire disagreement could have been avoided had the experiment integrated a more philosophical approach to the interpretation of its data.

Finally, I will provide a more concrete application of this exchange of disciplinary viewpoints to the case of addicted persons. Indeed, in the context of addiction studies, there is a temptation to resolve the problem of addiction and avoid the necessary discussion regarding the nature of voluntary actions and personal autonomy with clear-cut neuroreductionist evidence that negates all control that an addicted person may have over their behaviour. However, I will argue that in terms of policy discussions, more progress can be achieved by an interdisciplinary exchange between the neuroscience of addiction and the philosophy of action and that a more complex understanding of addiction that avoids simplistic and absolutist answers will be able to provide a more ethical account of responsibility for addicted persons.

Addiction as a Neurobiological Disease

The previous section unpacked some of the mechanisms by which the current paradigm of addiction as a brain disease was largely influenced by the NIDA's model. This brain disease model of addiction (BDMA) and its prominence in recent literature could easily give the impression that a consensus view on the aetiology of addiction as a neurobiological affliction has been reached by the wider neuroscientific community. However, it is important to point out that opposing views on the categorization of addiction as a chronic and relapsing brain disease exist (Heim, 2014). The general arguments against the BDMA stem from an inclusion of social experiences and lived phenomenological accounts of addicted persons (Schlimme, 2010), which at the very least problematize the view of human agency and action control present in the BDMA.

A common understanding of a disease is the idea of an underlying pathology causing observable symptoms of pain and suffering in a person. In defining a particular behavioural phenomenon as a disease, however, the social and personal ramifications in the wider culture cannot be ignored. Intrinsic to any view of a disease is the claim to need for care and the accompanying consideration of the person as a "patient" suffering passively from a combination of biologically determined factors. Thus, the view of addiction as a disease inevitably carries the conflation of an active choice (i.e., consumption of a substance) with a passive condition (i.e., being addicted to the substance). At least from a philosophical standpoint, I've already problematized this aspect of addiction: just how much of an actual choice is involved in an addictive action? How ought we to understand agency so that we may consider it "compromised" when a person is addicted?

Epistemically paradoxical though this may be, the aim of the neurobiological brain disease view is to precisely resolve this philosophical contradiction: the symptom of the disease is the continuous consumption of the substance, and the suffering of the ailment is the negative consequences (physical and emotional) that this produces. Describing addiction as a brain disease then likens it to something like Parkinson's Disease, wherein the involuntary movement and seizures of a patient are the consequence of deteriorating neural pathways. The appeal to an underlying brain pathology is then a useful tool in explaining the seeming paradox of addiction, to which I've alluded in previous chapters: why would a seemingly rational person make the evidently irrational choice of continuing to consume a substance they know to be detrimental to their health? The account of rationality as it pertains to an active choice has already been discussed in the second chapter, but another formulation can simply be: why would a person actively make a choice that is detrimental to their wellbeing? Herein the problematization of how exactly that choice is made, and whether it can be said that the choice is made freely comes into focus. It seems then that the project of the BDMA is to try and resolve this paradox of human rational choice, by conciliating the rejection of the philosophical claim that drug use is a compulsive behaviour which eradicates all possibility of agency within the individual while maintaining that addiction is a neurobiological disease which largely compromises that individual's agency.

Regardless of its characterization as a disease, an indisputable reality is that long-term consumption of psychoactive substances results in chronic effects on the brain (Koob et al., 1998), and few if any thinkers would argue against that. While the exact categorization of the emergent phenomenon that arises can be up for debate (Barata et al., 2019), learning cues and reward triggers in the brain do indeed become affected after long-term exposure to drugs which affect the levels of synaptic dopamine release. The most common interpretations have then tended towards the fact that certain drugs will trigger an overestimation of anticipated reward and will therefore carry an unusually strong motivational strength (Redish et al., 2008). Some authors postulate that over long enough periods of time, the "wanting" of the drug may even be distinct from the "liking" of it. Certain visual or environmental cues may trigger a particularly strong craving and thus motivate drug-seeking behaviour, regardless of whether or not the drug may even offer the same pleasure levels it once did (Holton & Berridge, 2013). This in-and-of-itself does not necessarily mean that the desire for the drug is irresistible, but rather that the intensity of the desire is unusually strong and incommensurate with other dopamine-centric levels of pleasure (e.g., food and sex). In this sense, and in view of the systematic reviews that attempt to define whether "substance abuse" can be understood as a medical diagnosis (Koob, 2006; Barata et al., 2019), it is understandable how this may be characterized as a pathological brain reward system. So, the question is posed: can this be enough to treat an addicted brain as suffering from a disease? And what would be the implications of doing so?

The neuroscience literature misses the crux of that argument, which requires an understanding of said argument through the lens of causal action theory. That crux lies in the inference of literal irresistibility from the affected underlying neurocircuitry in the brain, which would be the necessary argument to declare it a pathological state according to the medical consensus viewing addiction as compulsive drug use despite significant negative consequences impairing the health and wellbeing of the individual. Indeed, that a particular brain circuitry may deviate from the norm, due to its long-term exposure to psychoactive substances, would not be enough to declare it a pathological state. After all, virtually every action and/or consumable substance has an effect on the human brain. The question of pathology is in essence a question of what it means to have a "healthy" brain (i.e., to what extent does an abnormal brain circuitry qualify as a brain suffering from a disease?). After all, variation will always exist between individuals and some pathologies may simply be a commonly "different" type of brain. Instead, what is needed is a more nuanced understanding of what it means for a brain to function in a way that is expected with regards to common trigger cues involved in drug-relapsing scenarios (e.g., visual and other sensorial cues, persons associated with a memory of consumption, etc.), and then evaluate whether or not a different enough functioning given said cues qualifies as pathological; meaning in what way will a brain responding to a certain cue be no longer simply atypical, but in fact dysfunctional? What does a normal process of "liking" or "wanting" look like from a neurobiological standpoint? It is quite difficult to accurately paint a picture of a "normal" functioning brain, and some even argue that the neural changes manifested in addiction are part of a normal learning process of any brain (Lewis, 2015), an argument bolstered by the fact that certain studies show most people in their mid-30s tend to naturally quit their addictive habit (Heyman, 2009)[3]. An empirical observation of the effects that psychoactive substances have on the brain does yield an ever more detailed account of their effects on the neurocircuitry of the brain (Volkow et al., 2016), which at the very least must be taken into account when considering the degree to which a brain may be affected when exposed to long-term drug consumption.

Here it is worthwhile noting why an appeal to characterize addiction as a disease is both an ethical stance towards addicted persons and a logical conclusion from the genuinely puzzling circumstances surrounding most addicted persons' avowed experience of disliking and actively desiring to stop consuming the substance to which they are addicted. How else to explain the continuous use despite negative consequences if not by an explanation of compulsivity due to a neurobiological pathology? The dilemma both from a moral standpoint and an epistemic position is the conciliation between the acceptance that the condition may not be one of literal compulsion and that the changes in brain neurocircuitry may merely be a maladaptive response to long-term psychoactive substance abuse (Redish et al., 2008), with the fact that the condition of addiction ought to be treated for all intents and purposes as if it were a neurobiological illness, at least from a healthcare and treatment standpoint. This is a normative claim regarding the ethical treatment of persons suffering from addiction, and in order to support it we can either make an appeal to an ethical value judgement, in which we would argue that these people are indeed "suffering" and thus deserving of treatment; or we can make a more utilitarian argument that would appeal to the sense effectiveness of treatment instead of the ineffective cycle of penalization which further widens the social gaps, leading to increasingly poorer outcomes and thus increased rates of drug abuse. From either ethical approach, the stance remains that the condition of addiction would be better managed if treated as a public health phenomenon. A much more detailed argument for this strategy will be detailed in upcoming chapters, but for now, it is useful to keep it in mind as we focus on the neuroreductionist view of addiction.

This epistemic attitude, that we may not be able to definitively categorize addiction as pathological, but we should treat addicted persons as if it were, does not entail that neuroscientific research into the addicted brain cannot yield very useful information and provide an ever-clearer picture of what happens when a person is subjected to long-term substance abuse. Many aspects of the human mind and its relationship with specific behaviours such as addiction can indeed be explained through neuroscientific perspectives, to the point where it may be plausible that one day we will have a clear diagnostic statistical tool to assess whether a certain level of addiction qualifies as pathological (arbitrary and nebulous though that definition may one day be). Until that day, however, a normative stance has to be taken regarding the phenomenon and the gaps in our knowledge about said phenomenon that neuroscience cannot yet fill, and in taking that stance we must consider notions of freedom and choice that are relevant to the consideration of addiction as pathological.

What Neuroscience Cannot Tell Us about Action

In order to answer the paradox of continuous drug consumption, a first step might be to answer why some people decide to begin consuming the drug in the first place. It is clear that many reasons for taking drugs in the first place do not come from a pathological need to do so or a compulsion (Müller & Schumann, 2011). For many alcoholics, their first introduction to alcohol may have been through benign social settings, wherein the accepted form of drinking as a socializing facilitator may have led to chronic and problematic alcohol consumption. For other drugs, their initial use may have been through prescribed medicinal purposes, to counteract fatigue or pain, leading to a physical and/or psychological dependence. Another common reason for the beginning of drug abuse tends to be a means of coping with psychological stress or a way of self-medicating mental health issues like depression. Finally, a fairly benign reason to start using drugs is the curiosity that some young people may have to explore sensorial pleasure and the feeling of "being high". Yet their continuous use may lead to negative consequences eventually. This point is clearly laid out in accounts of people reporting diminishing returns of pleasure and joy from their once very pleasurable experience with drugs (Robinson et al., 2018), something which has been explained by an increased tolerance to the psychoactive effect of the drug on the brain (Volkow et al., 2016). This process of ever-diminishing returns may not in and of itself be a negative thing, were it not for the fact that it leads to higher and higher doses being sought and thus greater risk of overdoses.

It is then somewhat possible to understand the difficulty in pinpointing exactly at what point the negative consequences that drug use has on a person's life overwhelm the initial benefits. Indeed, this tipping point past which the costs of drug use outweigh the benefits can only be discovered by going past it, and no clear map of the brain function over time can tell us when that line will be crossed. This is where the external circumstances to drug use also become contributing factors to the continuation or cessation of drug use (e.g., sociocultural practices, criminalization policies, etc.) and contribute to the weighing of costs and consequences of continued drug use in a person's mind. Here the question now becomes: why would a person *continue* to seek illicit drugs? Considering that the costs, both tangible and intangible, of drug use outweigh whatever initial benefits the drug use may have had, and given most current policy stands against illicit addictive drug consumption, why would an addicted person continue to seek something the social, personal, and physical cost of which may outweigh its benefits? If we set aside the trap of neuroreductionist thinking for the moment, and avoid labelling addiction as a neurobiological disease, we must still grapple with the paradoxical phenomenon that is addictive behaviour for which no easy answer seems evident. Why indeed would a person continue to consume a substance they know is the cause of negative consequences? If literal compulsivity (i.e., an external force overriding one's internal volition) is not the answer, and we choose to have a more nuanced approach to understanding why an addicted person would continue their substance consumption, the answer must involve a philosophical understanding of what choice and "choosing to do something" involves.

Needless to say, this debate concerning the existence of free will in the human mind has been occupying philosophers and scientists alike for the better part of recorded human thought. It is unsurprising that new areas of research into the nature of human behaviour would have their say concerning this ageless question. Innovative experiments, such as the one conducted by Benjamin Libet in 1983, have integrated neuroscientific data and cognitive experiments into the free will debate, shedding light on new perspectives that deviate from the standard schools of thought on the free will discussion (Libet et al., 1983). This now-famous Libet experiment had participants look at a clock-like device, and sensors attached to their head to monitor their brain activity. As the participants were asked to spontaneously push a button and mentally record the moment at which they made that decision, the sensors could record their brain activity and compare the moment when they reportedly decided to press the button with the moment their brain actually "decided" to do so. The conclusion of this experiment was that an "unconscious" decision to press the button occurred before the participant was aware they were making such a choice (Libet et al., 1983). The findings of this experiment unsurprisingly created a lot of controversy due to its suggestion that at least certain facets of human action could be decisions made unconsciously. Many more experiments have been conducted since then, with notable variations adding to the purported idea of doubt regarding the ability of our consciousness to play a significant role in producing human behaviour (Wegner, 2003). Notably, and ironically enough, Libet himself cast doubt on his own reports regarding the conclusive nature of his findings about human will, and upon seeing the debate about free will his experiments had launched, commented that "*Speculations and theories not based on experimental data directly relevant to the experience of conscious intention have thus far provided little more than representations of personal philosophical viewpoints*" (Libet, 1985).

The challenges to these perspectives do not concern the data obtained, but rather the way in which it is analyzed. "*While most philosophers seem willing to agree that neuroscientific research has strong implications for the free will question, there is significant disagreement as to what the implications are*" (Morris, 2009).

Though instrumental in bringing a fresh neuroscientific perspective into the free will debate, ultimately the Libet experiments raised interesting critical questions about the relationship between consciousness and free will without providing the conclusive deterministic proof that some authors gleaned from it (Harris, 2009). Further questions about the nature of conscious versus unconscious will remain, as well as questions regarding the nature of the processes through which human beings make decisions. For the purposes of a case study on the special context of addictive behaviour, the question remains: are the chemical reactions we observe in the brain, that result from prolonged substance abuse and lead to unconscious decisions (e.g., consume an addictive substance), merely the underlying mechanisms of an altered human decision-making process or are they the cause of it?

There is an undeniable allure in providing tangible and observable new data to this age-old question, indeed. Neuroscience allows us to understand how certain parts of the brain correspond to specific actions and behaviours. But the philosophy of action is not focused on the locus of human action, but rather on the motivation and driving force behind it. Therein the difficulty in translating data obtained from electrical signals and chemical reactions in the brain into philosophical frameworks on human action and free will.

Explaining the "Puzzle of Addiction"

In her chapter "The Puzzle of Addiction", outlining what the possible answers to this "puzzle" may be, Hanna Pickard outlines five possible answers to the paradox of continuous substance abuse: the reason may be one of self-hatred and self-harm, either due to unprocessed psychological trauma or negative considerations of oneself, the issue of comorbidity with mental health issues include personality disorders that might contribute to an active participation in self-harming practices, of which drug abuse might be a part. "*Negative consequences only offer an incentive not to use drugs if a person values and cares about themselves. For people who don't, the costs of drug use may to some degree count as benefits, thereby solving the puzzle*" (Pickard, 2018).

A second explanation could be human misery, limited socio-economic opportunities, and poor mental health, wherein the environmental factors are a direct contribution to a person's decision to consume psychoactive substances in order to find an escapism avenue out of their condition. In difficult socio-economic circumstances, the same mental health problems might not so easily be solved through conventional methods of therapy or medical treatment, and thus the self-medication method of drugs is an often-reported entryway for people who suffer from chronic addiction.

One other explanation is a temporally myopic decision-making faculty, a staple of philosophical understandings for the paradox of time-discounted decision-making (Broome, 1994). This can essentially be boiled down to a lack of foresight on the part of first-time users and/or persons in the early stages of a substance addiction. The economic behavioural visualization of this phenomenon is a hyperbolic discount curve (i.e., the closer a reward appears in our timeline, the greater it seems), and we would simply apply a particularly steep hyperbolic curve to the case of addicted persons.

Pickard also proposes denial as a psychological defense mechanism, one which has been relatively ignored in the discussion concerning the justification and rationalization by addicted persons for their continued consumption of their addictive substance. Despite this, Pickard argues that the paradox of addiction could have a fairly simple explanation: addicted persons will simply deny the fact that there are negative consequences to their continued use. "*There is no puzzle why drug use persists if the costs associated with it are not known, and denial blocks this knowledge*" (Pickard, 2018).

Finally, the notion of self-identification can be understood as the conception that an addicted person may have of themselves, and here is where the trap of neuroreductionism rears its head once more.

> People who self-identify as addicts are therefore likely to persist in drug use almost by default – after all, that is what it is to be an addict. However, this may be further compounded if they view addiction according to the orthodox conception, as a neurobiological disease of compulsion.
>
> (Pickard, 2018)

The trap of an easy answer in the form of neurobiological disease views is manyfold, but one particular way is in the reinforcing of a deterministic worldview that might become a self-fulfilling prophecy in the mind of an addicted person, a phenomenon which has been clinically researched and tested (Racine et al., 2017).

From this perspective, the paradox of addictive behaviour becomes less of a problem to be solved via neuroscience data exclusively, and more of an epiphenomenon of compromised agency and free will that can greatly benefit from input stemming from a neuroscientific perspective. Indeed, scientific data provides useful ways of measuring, testing, and understanding aspects about human behaviour we might not have come to through philosophical introspection, but it is important to distinguish between a useful tool and a definitive proof.

The debate on free will is based on the assumption that it is a quality of unrestrained conscious control by an individual, with varying schools of thought differing on the matter of whether human beings actually possess such a capacity and its relation with a seemingly deterministic universe (determinism, compatibilism, and libertarianism). The case study of addiction offers a particularly interesting application of phenomenological inspections into notions of self-determination and self-agency (Schlimme, 2010), wherein the particular view of free will as a more or less permanent illusion is constantly fluctuating through states of intoxication and momentary sobriety. If indeed a neuroscientific approach to understanding brain functioning is helpful in having a clearer picture of what addiction looks like up close at the neural level, it gets us no closer to solving the paradox of why the mind *chooses* what it does in the throes of an addiction and therefore looks the way it does at that neural level.

If the neuroscience of addiction is a useful tool in understanding the mechanism of addictive behaviour as manifested in the brain but gets us no further to solving the paradox of why addicted persons engage in said addictive behaviour, why then has the brain disease view taken such a hold of the literature and community? And is there a useful use of this view in the context of further policy discussions?

Avoiding Easy Answers on Addictive Behaviour

As I detailed in the previous section, the BDMA as a neuroscientific paradigm has a specific history, and its social and political usefulness in promoting a reorientation of governmental attitudes towards addicted persons from a criminal justice strategy to a more public health-oriented strategy cannot be overstated.

Nevertheless, this usefulness does not come without some caveats. In their book "Brainwashed: The Seductive Appeal of Mindless Neuroscience", Satel and Lilienfeld argue that while the broader political support for increased funding for addiction studies and treatment options is certainly a worthwhile goal, the political utility of promoting a brain disease view of addiction and placing it on a comparable footing with other diseases such as Parkinson's and Alzheimer's comes at a cost: the neglecting of other non-neurobiological factors that come into play in addiction, all of which could equally benefit from funding and resources. Implying that the brain is the most useful level of analysis for addiction somehow equates it with a purely physical neurobiological illness. "*Such neurocentrism has clinical consequences, downplaying the underlying psychological and social reasons that drive drug use*" (Satel & Lilienfeld, 2013).

Faced with stigmatization fuelled by decades of anti-drug propaganda and harsh punitive measures, it would certainly be understandable to wish to err on the side of neurocentrism. After all, one might very well bite the utilitarian bullet and declare that if all human action is determined, we might as well medicalize the traits of human behaviour we wish to resolve. Yet this presumes once again at the very least an epistemic sure footing, with which some neuroscientists don't entirely agree. There is some scepticism regarding the value of findings in brain science, and the impossibility of explaining an emergent behavioural pattern such as addiction through ever-smaller levels of molecular observation (Kalant, 2010). There are concerns over the reliability of the images obtained through fMRI scans, which raises concern over the impulse to present these as evidence of the locus of the addiction problem reduced to merely a motivational impulse or a craving (indeed visible through lit-up images of brain scans). These concerns are usually exacerbated by the limited number of questions raised or concerns pitted against the ever-growing amount of funding invested in neuroscience research (Carter & Hall, 2011).

Social and clinical viewpoints might trade off epistemic coherence for beneficial treatment of addicted persons and the long-overdue removal of the stigmatization associated with addiction, but philosophers focused on action and volition may find that the neurobiological level of observation is not the most convenient place for notions regarding the agency of addicted persons. The focus on cognitive control of action by neuroscientific studies and the observation of pathophysiologic processes underlying addiction conforms with social conventions and folk understandings of voluntary control of behaviour by persons suffering from addiction, i.e. neuroscience for the most part agrees with folk understandings of cognitive regulatory power that controls actions based on conscious reasons. However, this is not something with which all philosophers entirely agree, either concerning the conscious exertion of will in general behaviour (Wegner, 2002) or in special contexts such as addiction (Hyman, 2005).

The neuroscientific focus on addiction studies also fails to address one major component of the philosophical view on the problem of addiction, the perceived "loss of control" by addicted persons in the throes of cravings. This lived experience in reality, though clinically observable, cannot be pinpointed in neurobiological terms, except as conclusions drawn from neurocircuits understood to underlie certain functions which have been disrupted by prolonged abnormal dopamine release spikes (Hyman, 2007). The focus on the notion of compulsion has come to be a defining trait in addiction studies and represents a significant change from previous medical conceptions that focused on dependence and physiological withdrawal symptoms, which were understood as positive motivating factors to action (i.e., actively taking the drug *in order to* avoid the withdrawal). Here, the concept of a compulsive act, i.e. the inability to avoid acting in a certain way, is much more coherent with the neurobiological picture of addiction as a brain disease, but represents a much more difficult case to be made in terms of the neuroscientific evidence aligning with theories of action about the actual possibility of an action being "involuntary" as opposed to simply "very difficult to resist" (Holton & Berridge, 2013).

Conclusion

The field of addiction studies would benefit from the continued and productive exchange between neuroscience and philosophy. Indeed, neuroscience as a discipline routinely addresses concepts such as free will, compulsion, and the nature of disease, concepts that benefit from a solid philosophical foundation and understanding; while conversely, any philosophical discussion equally benefits and produces more compelling arguments if they are constructed from the latest data provided by neuroscientific research, not to mention a solid understanding of it.

But the intertwinement of the two disciplines must go beyond mere dialogue and should produce a more transdisciplinary methodology of research. The two are in fact much more intimately conjoined than one might think. Taking the key concepts related to addiction studies, for example, we find that free will, compulsion, and something like the very nature of what is a disease, are notions that cannot be fully studied from a neuroscientific point of view, without a comprehensive understanding of their philosophical implications first. One example I discussed here is the fact that some very compelling arguments for addiction to be a distinct type of disease rely on the philosophical definition of "disease" as something involving involuntary and non-autonomous action (Peele, 1999).

Problematic behaviour, i.e. irrational and/or troublesome, has long been a subject of interest for philosophers, as well as scientists focused on human behaviour (e.g., psychologists and, more recently, neuroscientists). Concepts such as free will, self-control, and impulsivity, have been at the centre of addiction studies from a philosophical point of view, and recent advances in neuroscience, specifically in the past few decades, have contributed greatly to a better understanding of the brain mechanisms underlying phenomena such as "conscious decisions" to perform an action (Libet et al., 1983), and our ability to control said actions. However, many philosophers have been sceptical about the conclusions one ought to draw from these experiments (Mele, 2006; Dennett, 2003), and one could argue that the problem stems from the gaps between what science can conclusively say and the areas more commonly associated with philosophical inquiry, for example, human volition and responsibility. Conversely, the philosophical approach may sometimes be criticized for remaining too abstract and ignoring concrete evidence towards a definitive answer to what may have at first appeared to be a metaphysical and unknowable truth (e.g., do human beings possess the ability to perform undetermined actions?).

As the previous section on the neuroscientific advances on addiction studies suggested, the NIDA paradigm promotes the idea that addiction can be best categorized as a brain disease and that behaviour stemming from an addicted mind is compulsive and beyond the conscious control of the subject. Philosophers have put forth arguments against this claim by providing evidence that rewards, extenuating circumstances, and contextual support, all contribute to behaviour modulation by addicted persons. The result is a problematic definition of concepts such as "compulsivity", "volition", and "self-control". While one camp may simply dismiss the other as an erroneous interpretation of data, and vice-versa, either of those scenarios would seem to suggest an objective truth regarding human behaviour in terms of volition and control, which in and of itself is a philosophical postulate. The notion of free will and whether specific case studies of addiction may provide examples for either camp of that debate seems like a perfect case of a philosophical approach providing necessary and worthwhile contributions to a field of scientific research into metaphysical problems, especially as they pertain to matters of policy dealing with the responsibility of addicted persons for their actions.

This realm of policy pertaining to addicted persons is precisely where I turn to next. So far, I have established a solid philosophical foundation for the understanding of action theory norms and what addictive actions represent in terms of deviations from those norms. The neuroscientific perspective has then been introduced in order to have a better sense of the state of the art of our understanding of *how* addictive action is manifested in the brain. This perspective is useful in the development of a paradigm that defines addiction as a disease. I have, in this chapter, attempted to problematize this definition of a brain disease through the interaction and dialogue between both the neuroscience and the philosophy of addiction, so that a new transdisciplinary methodology of addiction research may be developed and in turn our conceptions of free will, agency, and compulsion in the context of addictive behaviour may be more nuanced. The task now is to see why such a methodology is necessary in order to better shape our governmental attitudes towards addicted persons. In the following chapters, I will situate my discussion of addiction within the legal conception of responsibility and liability as related to addiction. This will in turn lead to a discussion of the evolution of said legal conception of addicted persons' responsibility, the crux of which is my thesis regarding how policies ought to be constructed to deal with addicted persons more ethically.

Notes

1 Though not entirely in the realm of the neurobiological effect of a drug, the different modes of administration may indirectly lead to barriers of use and hence to diminished addiction rates. Think of the coughing and discomfort associated with smoking tobacco. Strong social pressure and a certain tenacity is needed to overcome this discomfort and continue smoking, which takes time and thus delays the point of addiction to the substance. The absence of these barriers for drinking alcohol, for example, help in understanding the higher addiction rates among young people for alcohol than tobacco (EMCDDA, 2014).

2 It is important to note that some drugs may have the opposite effect. Meaning a higher sensitization to the substance, leading to stronger cravings though not a higher tolerance level. Due to this higher sensitization, some chronic users may experience epiphenomenal symptoms unrelated to a direct neurobiological effect, such as paranoia (Satel et al., 1991).

3 This argument is made by Gene Heyman in Chapter 4 of his book "Addiction: A Disorder of Choice" (2009), wherein he argues that co-morbidity with other psychiatric illnesses contributes to most addicted persons remaining addicted past that age.

References

American Psychiatric Association. (2013). *Diagnostic and Statistical Manual of Mental Disorders (DSM-5)*. American Psychiatric Pub.

Barata, P.C., Oliveira, C.F.P., Castro, S.L.de, & Mota, A.M.P.R.da. (2019). A Systematic Review on Substance Addiction: Medical diagnosis or Morality Flaw? *The European Journal of Psychiatry*, *33*(4), 143–151. https://doi.org/10.1016/j.ejpsy.2019.07.001

Beck, A.T., Wright, F.D., & Newman, C.F. (1992). Cocaine Abuse. In *Comprehensive Casebook of Cognitive Therapy* (pp. 185–192). Boston, MA: Springer.

Berke, J.D., & Hyman, S.E. (2000). Addiction, Dopamine, and the Molecular Mechanisms of Memory. *Neuron*, *25*(3), 515–532.

Berridge, K.C. (2004). Motivation Concepts in Behavioral Neuroscience. *Physiology & Behavior*, *81*(2), 179–209.

Berridge, K.C., & Robinson, T.E. (1998). What is the Role of Dopamine in Reward: Hedonic Impact, Reward Learning, or Incentive Salience?. *Brain Research Reviews*, *28*(3), 309–369.

Broome, J. (1994). Discounting the Future. *Philosophy & Public Affairs*, *23*(2), 128–156. Retrieved May 25, 2021, from http://www.jstor.org/stable/2265483

Buchman, D.Z., Skinner, W., & Illes, J. (2010). Negotiating the Relationship Between Addiction, Ethics, and Brain Science. *AJOB Neuroscience*, *1*(1), 36–45.

Carter, A., & Hall, W. (2011). *Addiction Neuroethics: The Promises and Perils of Neuroscience Research on Addiction*. Cambridge, UK: Cambridge University Press.

Cloninger, C.R., Sigvardsson, S., Gilligan, S.B., von Knorring, A.L., Reich, T., & Bohman, M. (1988). Genetic Heterogeneity and the Classification of Alcoholism. *Advances in Alcohol & Substance Abuse*, *7*(3–4), 3–16.

Cooper, J.R., Bloom, F.E., & Roth, R.H. (1996). Cellular Foundation of Neuropharmacology. In *The Biochemical Basis of Neuropharmacology* (7th ed., pp. 9–48). New York: Oxford University Press.

Courtwright, D.T. (2010). The NIDA Brain Disease Paradigm: History, Resistance and Spinoffs. *BioSocieties*, *5*(1), 137–147. https://doi.org/10.1057/biosoc.2009.3

Dennett, D. (2003). *Freedom Evolves* (p. 232). Viking Press.

Di Chiara, G. (2000). Role of Dopamine in the Behavioural Actions of Nicotine Related to Addiction. *European Journal of Pharmacology*, *393*(1–3), 295–314.

Di Chiara, G., & Imperato, A. (1988). Drugs Abused by Humans Preferentially Increase Synaptic Dopamine Concentrations in the Mesolimbic System of Freely Moving Rats. *Proceedings of the National Academy of Sciences*, *85*(14), 5274–5278.

Dowell, D., Haegerich, T.M., & Chou, R. (2016). CDC Guideline for Prescribing Opioids for Chronic Pain—United States, 2016. *JAMA*, *315*(15), 1624–1645.

Drug Enforcement Administration. (2009). Methamphetamine. http://www.usdoj.gov/dea/concern/meth.html

EMCDDA. (2014). European Drug Report: Trends and Developments.

Fingarette, H. (1988). *Heavy Drinking: The Myth of Alcoholism as a Disease*. Berkeley: University of California Press.

Harris, S. (2009). *Free Will* (p. 9). New York: Free Press.

Heim, D. (2014). Addiction: Not Just Brain Malfunction. *Nature*, *507*(7490), 40–40.

Heyman G. (2009). *Addiction: A Disorder of Choice*. Cambridge: Harvard University Press.

Holton, R., & Berridge, K. (2013). Addiction Between Compulsion and Choice. In N. Levy (Ed.), *Addiction and Self-Control* (pp. 239–268). Oxford University Press. https://doi.org/10.1093/acprof:oso/9780199862580.003.0012

Hyman, S.E. (1996). Addiction to Cocaine and Amphetamine. *Neuron*, *16*(5), 901–904.

Hyman, S.E. (2005). Addiction: A Disease of Learning and Memory. *American Journal of Psychiatry*, *162*(8), 1414–1422.

Hyman, S.E. (2007). The Neurobiology of Addiction: Implications for Voluntary Control of Behavior. *The American Journal of Bioethics*, *7*(1), 8–11. https://doi.org/10.1080/15265160601063969

Hyman, S.E., Malenka, R.C., & Nestler, E.J. (2006). Neural Mechanisms of Addiction: The Role of Reward-Related Learning and Memory. *Annual Review of Neuroscience*, *29*, 565–598.

Johnson, B.A. (2005). Recent Advances in the Development of Treatments for Alcohol and Cocaine Dependence. *CNS Drugs*, *19*(10), 873–896.

Kalant, H. (2010). What Neurobiology Cannot Tell Us About Addiction. *Addiction*, *105*, 780–789.

Kalivas, P.W., & Volkow, N.D. (2005). The Neural Basis of Addiction: A Pathology of Motivation and Choice. *American Journal of Psychiatry*, *162*(8), 1403–1413.

Koob, G.F. (1992a). Dopamine, Addiction and Reward. In *Seminars in Neuroscience* (Vol. 4, No. 2, pp. 139–148). Academic Press.

Koob, G.F. (1992b). Drugs of Abuse: Anatomy, Pharmacology and Function of Reward Pathways. *Trends in Pharmacological Sciences*, *13*, 177–184.

Koob, G.F. (1996). Drug Addiction: The Yin and Yang of Hedonic Homeostasis. *Neuron*, *16*(5), 893–896.

Koob, G.F., & Le Moal, M. (2008). Addiction and the Brain Antireward System. *Annual Review of Psychology*, *59*, 29–53.

Koob, G.F., & Simon, E.J. (2009). The Neurobiology of Addiction: Where We Have Been and Where We Are Going. *Journal of Drug Issues*, *39*(1), 115–132.

Koob, G.F., & Volkow, N.D. (2010). Neurocircuitry of Addiction. *Neuropsychopharmacology*, *35*(1), 217–238.

Koob, G.F., Sanna, P.P., & Bloom, F. E. (1998). Neuroscience of Addiction. *Neuron*, *21*(3), 467–476. https://doi.org/10.1016/S0896-6273(00)80557-7

Koob, G.F. (2006), The Neurobiology of Addiction: A Neuroadaptational View Relevant for Diagnosis. *Addiction*, *101*, 23–30. https://doi-org.ezproxy.is.ed.ac.uk/10.1111/j.1360-0443.2006.01586.x

Kreek, M.J., Nielsen, D.A., Butelman, E.R., & LaForge, K.S. (2005). Genetic Influences on Impulsivity, Risk Taking, Stress Responsivity and Vulnerability to Drug Abuse and Addiction. *Nature Neuroscience*, *8*(11), 1450–1457.

Leshner, A.I. (1997). Addiction Is a Brain Disease, and It Matters. *Science*, *278*(5335), 45–47. https://doi.org/10.1126/science.278.5335.45

Levine, H.G. (1978). The Discovery of Addiction. Changing Conceptions of Habitual Drunkenness in America. *Journal of Studies on Alcohol*, *39*(1), 143–174. https://doi.org/10.15288/jsa.1978.39.143

Levy, N. (2010). Addiction and Compulsion. In *A Companion to the Philosophy of Action* (pp. 267–273). John Wiley & Sons, Ltd., https://doi.org/10.1002/9781444323528.ch34

Lewis, M. (2015). *The Biology of Desire: Why Addiction is not a Disease*. New York, NY: Perseus Books Group

Li, T.K., & McBride, W.J. (1995). Pharmacogenetic Models of Alcoholism. *Clinical Neuroscience* (New York, NY), *3*(3), 182.

Libet, B. (1985). Unconscious Cerebral Initiative and the Role of Conscious Will in Voluntary Action. *Behavioral and Brain Sciences*, *8*(4), 529–539. doi:10.1017/S0140525X00044903

Libet, B., Libet, B., Gleason, C.A., Wright, E.W., & Pearl, D.K. (1983). Time of Conscious Intention to Act in Relation to Onset of Cerebral Activity (Readiness-Potential). *Brain*, *106*(3), 623–642.

Luborsky, L., Woody, G.E., Hole, A.V., & Velleco, A. (1995). Supportive-Expressive Dynamic Psychotherapy for Treatment of Opiate Drug Dependence.

Marlatt, G.A., & Donovan, D.M. (Eds.). (2005). *Relapse Prevention: Maintenance Strategies in the Treatment of Addictive Behaviors*. Guilford Press.

Mele, A.R. (2006). *Free Will and Luck*. Oxford University Press.

Morris, Stephen G. (2009). The Impact of Neuroscience on the Free Will Debate. *Florida Philosophical Review*, *9*(2), 56. http://philosophy.cah.ucf.edu/fpr/files/9_2/morris.pdf

Müller, C.P., & Schumann, G. (2011). Drugs as Instruments: A New Framework for Non-Addictive Psychoactive Drug Use. *The Behavioral and Brain Sciences*, *34*(6), 293–310. https://doi.org/10.1017/S0140525X11000057

Nestler, E.J., & Aghajanian, G.K. (1997). Molecular and Cellular Basis of Addiction. *Science*, *278*(5335), 58–63.

Newman, C.F. (2001). *Cognitive Therapy of Substance Abuse*. Guilford Press.

O'Brien, C.P. (1996). Drug Addiction and Drug Abuse. In: Hardman, J.G., Limbird, L., (Eds.) *Goodman and Gilman's The Pharmacologic Basis of Therapeutics* (9th ed., pp. 557–577). New York: McGraw-Hill.

O'Malley, S.S., Jaffe, A.J., Chang, G., Rode, S., Schottenfeld, R., Meyer, R.E., & Rounsaville, B. (1996). Six-month Follow-Up of Naltrexone and Psychotherapy for Alcohol Dependence. *Archives of General Psychiatry*, *53*(3), 217–224.

O'Connor, T. (2005). Freedom with a Human Face. In *Agency and Causation in the Human Sciences* (pp. 111–124). Mentis.

Olds, M.E., & Milner, P. (1954). Positive Reinforcement Produced by Electrical Stimulation of Septal Area and Other Regions of the Rat Brain. *Journal of Comparative and Physiological Psychology*, *47*, 419–427.

Peele, S. (1999). *Diseasing of America: How We Allowed Recovery Zealots and the Treatment Industry to Convince Us We are Out of Control*. Prentice Hall.

Pickard, H. (2018). The Puzzle of Addiction. In H. Pickard & S.H. Ahmed (Eds.), *The Philosophy and Science of Addiction* (pp. 9–22). New York: Routledge.

Pierce, R.C., & Kumaresan, V. (2006). The Mesolimbic Dopamine System: The Final Common Pathway for the Reinforcing Effect of Drugs of Abuse?. *Neuroscience & Biobehavioral Reviews*, *30*(2), 215–238.

Racine, E., Sattler, S., & Escande, A. (2017). Free Will and the Brain Disease Model of Addiction: The Not So Seductive Allure of Neuroscience and Its Modest Impact on the Attribution of Free Will to People with an Addiction. *Frontiers in Psychology*, 8. https://doi.org/10.3389/fpsyg.2017.01850

Redish, A.D., Jensen, S., & Johnson, A. (2008). A Unified Framework for Addiction: Vulnerabilities in the Decision Process. *Behavioral and Brain Sciences*, *31*(4), 415–437. https://doi.org/10.1017/S0140525X0800472X

Reich, T., Edenberg, H.J., Goate, A., Williams, J.T., Rice, J.P., Van Eerdewegh, P., et al. (1998). Genome-wide Search for Genes Affecting the Risk for Alcohol Dependence. *American Journal of Medical Genetics*, *81*(3), 207–215.

Rhee, S.H., Hewitt, J.K., Young, S.E., Corley, R.P., Crowley, T.J., & Stallings, M.C. (2003). Genetic and Environmental Influences on Substance Initiation, Use, and Problem Use in Adolescents. *Archives of General Psychiatry*, *60*(12), 1256–1264.

Robbins, T., Cardinal, R.N., DiCiano, P., Halligan, P.W., Hellemans, K., Lee, J., & Everitt, B.J. (2007). Neuroscience of Drugs and Addiction. In *Drugs and the Future* (pp. 11–87). Academic Press.

Robinson, M.J., Robinson, T.E., & Berridge, K.C. (2018). The Current Status of the Incentive Sensitization Theory of Addiction. In *The Routledge Handbook of Philosophy and Science of Addiction* (pp. 351–361). Routledge.

Satel, S.L., Southwick, S.M., & Gawin, F.H. (1991). Clinical Features of Cocaine-Induced Paranoia. *The American Journal of Psychiatry*.

Satel, S., & Lilienfeld, S.O. (2013). *Brainwashed: The Seductive Appeal of Mindless Neuroscience*. Basic Books.

Schlimme, J.E. (2010). Addiction and Self-determination: A Phenomenological Approach. *Theoretical Medicine and Bioethics*, *31*(1), 49–62. https://doi.org/10.1007/s11017-010-9134-0

Schultz, W. (1998). Predictive Reward Signal of Dopamine Neurons. *Journal of Neurophysiology*, *80*(1), 1–27.

Stephens, L.G., & Graham, G. (2009). An Addictive Lesson: A Case Study in Psychiatry as Cognitive Neuroscience. In M. Broome and L. Bortolotti (Eds.), *Psychiatry as Cognitive Neuroscience*. Oxford: Oxford University Press.

Thomasson, H.R., Edenberg, H.J., Crabb, D.W., Mai, X-L., Jerome, P.E., Li, T-K., Wang, S.P., Liu, Y.T., Lu, R.B., & Yin, S.J. (1991). Alcohol and Aldehyde Genotypes and Alcoholism in Chinese Men. *American Journal of Human Genetics*, *48*, 677–681.

Thomasson, H.R., Zeng, D., Mai, X.-L., McGarvey, S., Deka, R., & Li, T.-K. (1994). Population Distribution of ADH2 and ALDH2 Alleles. *Alcoholism: Clinical and Experimental Research*, *18*, 60A.

Volkow, N.D., & Fowler, J.S. (2000). Addiction, A Disease of Compulsion and Drive: Involvement of the Orbitofrontal Cortex. *Cerebral Cortex* (New York, N.Y.: 1991), *10*(3), 318–325. https://doi.org/10.1093/cercor/10.3.318

Volkow, N.D., & Koob, G. (2015). Brain Disease Model of Addiction: Why is it so Controversial? *The Lancet Psychiatry*, *2*(8), 677–679. https://doi.org/10.1016/S2215-0366(15)00236-9

Volkow, N.D., Koob, G.F., & McLellan, A.T. (2016). Neurobiologic Advances from the Brain Disease Model of Addiction. *New England Journal of Medicine*, *374*(4), 363–371. https://doi.org/10.1056/NEJMra1511480

Volpicelli, J.R., Alterman, A.I., Hayashida, M., & O'Brien, C.P. (1992). Naltrexone in the Treatment of Alcohol Dependence. *Archives of General Psychiatry*, *46*, 876–880.

Wegner, D.M. (2002). *The Illusion of Conscious Will.* Cambridge, MA: The MIT Press.

Wegner, D.M. (2003). The Mind's Best Trick: How We Experience Conscious Will. *Trends in Cognitive Sciences*, 7(2), 65–69.

Wilkinson, P., Van Dyke, C., Jatlow, P., Barash, P., & Byck, R. (1980). Intranasal and Oral Cocaine Kinetics. *Clinical Pharmacology and Therapeutics*, *27*, 386–394.

Wise, R.A. (1978). Catecholamine Theories of Reward: A Critical Review. *Brain Research*, *152*, 215–247.

Chapter 4

UK Drug Policy

Its History and Tensions in Criminal Responsibility

Introduction

In the previous chapters, I have focused on the being qua being of addiction, i.e. the behavioural phenomenon of *being* addicted, its underlying neurobiology, and its consequences for our understanding of compulsive action and compromised agency. These chapters have focused on the contrasting of the distinct conceptualizations of addiction. This section of my book will now concern how those conceptualizations inform and shape UK drug policy. The objective of these two final chapters is to turn the focus on to the critical analysis of drug policy and the political constructs that frame said policies aimed at dealing with the harms related to addiction.

In order to begin this section, a brief overview of where the UK is situated with regard to drug use and drug policy is warranted. The United Kingdom ranks as one of the nations with the highest levels of drug use for cocaine and opioids and ranks #4 in a list of European countries' drug-induced mortality rates (EMCDDA, 2019). A brief history of the drug control legislation in the United Kingdom would highlight the Misuse of Drugs Act of 1971 as a milestone legislative event, when the system to classify drugs according to their perceived harmfulness was set up, and which established the Advisory Council on the Misuse of Drugs (ACMD), a council tasked with providing evidence-based scientific research and policy proposals to the UK government (Reuter & Stevens, 2007). Given the relatively high incidence of drug use and drug-related harm in the United Kingdom today, it would be fair to say that the policies established to deal with the "drug problem" have not been successful during the decades since they were put into effect.

As Alex Stevens writes, "*The debate on drugs is dominated by one, endlessly recurring argument. Should drugs be legal or prohibited?*" (Stevens, 2011, p. 1). This debate and the rhetoric of the "War on Drugs", a term for the global campaign led against illicit drug use and coined at the beginning of the 1970s, revolve around the idea that illicit drug use is inherently immoral. The problem is that deciding which drug is illicit has historically been a

DOI: 10.4324/9781003582908-5

choice made independent of the chemical properties of the psychoactive substance in question, with "illicit drugs" encompassing a vast range of substances with different chemical properties that have as much in common with their legal counterparts as they do with other illicit substances. The only relevant distinguishing factor between licit and illicit drugs is *ipso facto* their legal status (Holland, 2020).

Reviewing the legislative history around drug control in the United Kingdom gives us a better idea of how and why certain substances have become illicit, while others remain perfectly legal. This provides the necessary context for the distinct types of policy constructs that I will focus on in the following chapter. These constructs have specific histories and in order to assess how a strategy rooted in harm reduction is more effective and ethical in its treatment of addicted persons, it is worthwhile understanding the history of why consumption of certain substances has become criminalized over the centuries. And the short answer is that such delineations between licit and illicit substances have never been clear and neat. In fact, they have evolved and depended largely on socio-political circumstances, rather than scientific research on which substances are more harmful.

In reviewing this legislative history, I will attempt to provide a critical and ethical analysis of the conceptual basis that underlies the UK drug policy framework. I will largely adhere to Toby Seddon's work on the historical narratives that have emerged through milestone legislative events which have revised the conceptual basis for the criminal law approach to drug control. I will then provide an assessment of the sociopolitical impact that these policies have had in the scene of substance abuse in the United Kingdom. Finally, I will look at the law's conception of responsibility and consider the attitude that the law has and ought to have towards compulsivity and/or mitigating excuses that challenge the normal presumption of intentionality in criminal acts.

The overhaul of an entire justice system concerning such a vast and heterogeneous class of criminal behaviour is a daunting task, and I do not pretend to do so here. However, I do hope to offer some thoughts on the ethical considerations needed for proposed legal and policy reforms aimed at ameliorating the justice system's approach to dealing with addicted persons convicted of drug-related crimes. In doing so, it will allow me to focus on the final preliminary question of my book: What public health policy strategies are better suited to dealing with addicted persons compromised capacity for agency and responsibility?

Conceptualizing Drug Policy as a Problem of Liberal Governance

Human civilization has always struggled with the issue of how best to deal with addicted persons through legal and policy measures. And as liberal as societies may have become, hardly any nation-state gives free rein to the flow of psychoactive substances in the open market. Regulations range from the mere accurate indication of the chemical makeup of a substance (e.g., caffeine) to the complete prohibition on the production and trade of a substance (e.g., heroin). The social and political issues that emanate from this problem of regulation are varied and complex (Room, 2006).

However, although the problem of controlling and regulating psychoactive substances is indeed ancient, for the purposes of this chapter I will focus on the *problematization of addiction*, and consider a historical genealogical study of the legislative attempts to govern it, wherein I will take addiction as a social problem to be solved, which in reality dates back to a time much earlier than the time of Hammurabi. Indeed, though the consumption of psychoactive substances may be as old as civilization itself (Guerra-Doce, 2015), the notion of a certain type of substances, or rather a certain type of consumers of such substances, being *a problem* for society dates back to the beginning of the industrial age and its effect on the conception of the citizen within the liberal state (Seddon, 2009).

In Robin Room's paper "Addiction Concepts and International Control" (2006), he provides a historical analysis of how the concept of addiction came to be applied to alcohol consumers first and consumers of other types of psychoactive substances soon after. This problematization of the consumption of psychoactive substances emerged, according to Room's view, from a need to conciliate the paradox of a need for sobriety in the new mechanical practices that represented the majority of the workforce's occupations upon the advent of the Industrial Revolution, with the economic need for the substances to be widely consumed as part of the commodities trade upon which most colonial empires were built (alcohol, tobacco, tea, opium, chocolate, and sugar).

This historical context serves as a background for my present discussion, and I provide it in order to situate the problem of addiction as a problem of liberal governance. To understand what may have been the difficulties in solving this problem so far, and indeed there have been difficulties as I will try to demonstrate in my distinction between policy-construction frameworks, it is imperative that we understand the epistemological dissonance within the philosophical conception of addiction, and specifically the behaviour of addicted persons, in the policy-construction frameworks that have not embraced the conception of addiction as a brain disease. Rather, it is their traditional view of addicted persons as agents making irrational choices[1], and its erroneous philosophical conception of the addicted person's condition which I will argue, in the following chapter, is at the root of the difference in the effectiveness of policy constructs dealing with addiction.

Understanding this dissonance is key in constructing the ethical argument on top of the "effectiveness" argument. Indeed, a report from the United Nations High Commissioner for Human Rights highlighted in 2015 the main areas in which drug policies had violated human rights throughout the world. These included arbitrary arrests and poor treatment of addicted persons, unjustified use of the death penalty for drug offenses in certain countries, unethical clinical treatment of patients, racial discriminatory behaviour in law enforcement practices, denial of life-saving treatment for people at risk of drug overdose, excessive rates of incarceration for minor drug offences, and little access to opioid derivatives and other medicine used in pain management (UN, 2015). Understanding the evolving international debate on the best use of policy to tackle drug use goes hand in hand with addressing these ethical concerns over human rights violations and the overall treatment of persons suffering from addiction. That is the fundamental postulate of these two final chapters: a more effective type of drug policy must be understood in terms of it being more ethical as well.

The dissonance in policy constructs is made evident in their different effectiveness in reducing harms related to drug consumption. This dissonance comes from the different conceptualization of addiction as a disorder that compromises a person's agential capabilities. Thus, the philosophy of action, and more specifically the realm of causal action theory, is what has provided me with the necessary conceptual tools to better analyze this dissonance in policy constructs. I have situated this book and its section concerned with philosophical notions, within the work of Donald Davidson and his paper "Actions, Reasons, and Causes" (1963), in which he establishes the idea of rationalization as the mental exercise which in turn provides a sufficient causal explanation for actions. This context serves as the foundation for the present discussion regarding the conceptions of the actions taken by addicted persons in different policy constructs. Davidson's work on intentionality serves as a way of constructing a dual conception of addictive behaviour, both as obviously intentional in the literal sense and yet capable of being analyzed through the prism of a compulsive disorder. Understanding the addicted person's experience of feeling a compulsion to behave in a way that they do not want allows for a certain akratic conception of addicted persons' actions. In understanding Davidson's view on the possibility of akratic action (Heather & Segal, 2013), I will attempt to extrapolate such a conception to a policy construct aiming to treat addicted persons' behaviour as part of a medical disorder (i.e., a brain disease) and postulate that such an understanding can explain why harm reduction strategies are more effective in dealing with addiction problems in society.

It is important to note that I do not mean to make a distinction between policy constructs by attributing a distinct disciplinary perspective to each, for example E-L constructs adopting a philosophical conception of addiction while L-E constructs are exclusively neuroscientific constructs. Rather I mean to argue that the brain disease paradigm is in itself a specific philosophical position concerning the behaviour of addicted persons and the way in which it is most useful to conceive of them. The necessity for a section dedicated to causal action theory is precisely in order to introduce the idea that categorizing certain types of behaviour as resulting from a medical disorder is distinct from conceiving of such behaviour as emanating from irrationality or immoral choices, the postulate implicit in E-L policy constructs. Hence, both the philosophical and neuroscientific summaries in previous chapters of this paper will serve as a context for the discussion about policy constructs and their varying levels of effectiveness in reducing the harm of addiction.

Though it is by no means an original thought to say that addiction as a phenomenon is inherently multidimensional and that its study requires an interdisciplinary approach, I will suggest that even within a specific subset of a disciplinary perspective inquiry into addiction, i.e. social policy analysis, the inclusion of a philosophical and neuroscientific perspective is not only beneficial but even necessary in order to make coherent policy recommendations. This has been the case in some accounts of how best to conceptualize addiction from an epistemological standpoint:

> Work that draws on the ontological turn and, to some extent, the ongoing discussions around the merits and challenges raised by BDMA, make apparent the need for this line of inquiry: "Things" that in the past we have taken as fundamental truths, and the source of the activities of interest to us, have themselves become outcomes of yet more fundamental and taken for granted activities.
>
> (Hellman, 2021, p.5)

The emergence in recent years of a "biopsychosocial" approach to addiction policy recommendations is indeed in line with this point (Buchman et al., 2010), and as I will attempt to demonstrate in this book, the effectiveness of drug policy constructs depends to some degree upon their philosophical conceptions of addicted persons and their behaviour.

A Brief History of UK Drug Policy

Drug policy strategies can be defined as the patterns of legislation and governmental actions that are focused towards the control of drug consumption by the population, as well as all the correlated harms that are associated with drug use in society. Over the course of nearly 150 years, the United Kingdom has had a long and evolving history of such policy strategies. As I have mentioned before, I place my critical analysis of UK drug policy within the narrative established by Toby Seddon's "A History of Drugs: Drugs and Freedom in the Liberal Age" (2009), in which a narrative of the evolution of UK drug policy can be established through key legislative events throughout recent centuries.

Beginning with the Pharmacy Act of 1868, which saw the first regulation of poisons and dangerous substances, this was a first attempt to regulate who could legally sell such substances (i.e., licensed pharmacists). Up until then, there was very little control over the legality of drug use and commercialization. Concoctions derived from opium and coca leaves were readily available and widely sold all over the country. The Pharmacy Act marked an initial phase introducing legal controls over the sale of these substances.

A second phase, which saw the creation of a national system of control, was brought about due to increasing concerns over the use of cocaine and other drugs by soldiers returning from the battlefield of World War I (Spear and Mott, 1993). This was compounded by fear and paranoia surrounding the use of drugs by immigrants and ethnic minorities in the cities, especially London (Kohn, 2001). Within this system, known as the "British System", cocaine and heroin could be prescribed by attending physicians to patients who were "dependent" on the drug, while the distribution and sale of said drugs were criminalized.

This system was upended in the 1960s, following an increase in the amount of prescribed heroin by doctors, which found its way into the illegal market. Additionally, an increase in the use of cannabis, amphetamines, and LSD led to a third phase of regulation that increased control of these substances. This was accompanied in the 1970s by the introduction of methadone as an alternative method of treatment for persons addicted to heroin (Strang and Sheridan, 2006). It was around this time that the Misuse of Drugs Act (MDA) combined the various measures that had been introduced through previous legislation and established the classification system by which drugs are still categorized to this day.

The fourth, and current, phase of legislative control can be said to have begun in 1991 with the Criminal Justice Act, which allowed for the condition of attending drug treatment to be attached to a probation order. This marks the first legal attempt to integrate public health policy with criminal justice approaches, which ushered in the current framework for legislation which tries to minimize the separation between medical and punitive responses.

While the historical narrative of UK drug policy that I have chosen to follow in this book can be summarized in a few significant legislative events (Seddon, 2009), it can equally be described in more abstract distinct eras, such as an era when policy was focused on reducing supply in the 1980s, an era when policy was focused on reducing demand in the 1990s, and the present era when the emphasis of policy has been more focused on harm reduction since the 2000s (Bennett & Holloway, 2005). One significant and era-defining legislative event, however, was the Misuse of Drugs Act of 1971 (MDA), which established the drug classification system which is still in place today, a remarkably stable and immovable charter despite much criticism and developments in UK drug policy thinking for the past 50 years.

The MDA of 1971 exemplified the "British System", an approach to drug policy wherein the locus of the drug problem and its purported solution seemed to be an overlap between the criminal justice system and the medical profession (Berridge, 1984). This overlap originated from the time period immediately after World War I, when the Home Office in the United Kingdom tried to adopt a similar system to that of the United States, which relied entirely on a penal approach and sanctions to both users and medical doctors for over-prescribing opiates such as morphine and heroin (Strang & Gossop, 1994). Sometime later, the Rolleston Committee of 1926 distinguished between the concept of addiction and "drug abuse", which was an argument for the "medicalization" of addicted persons, and thus a push for their condition to be treated instead of punished. This event culminated in the involvement of the medical profession in UK drug policy (South, 1997) and thus created the overlap between criminal persecution and medical treatment which defines the "British system" (Stimson & Lart, 1994). A system, however, that many have described as having an asymmetric power and influence structure, with public health initiatives and treatment efforts established within a framework set up by the Home Office, which is largely punishment and enforcement-oriented (Stevens, 2007; Seddon et al., 2008).

This framework, and the underlying motivating philosophy behind the Home Office's attitude toward drug control, is therefore one that conceives of drug consumption as a deviant practice (either criminally deviant or medically deviant), which in turn opposes or completely ignores a third and more transcendental political opinion that would view drug use as inherently unproblematic. Some of the latest parliamentary proposals for the reformation of the Misuse of Drugs Act of 1971 are aligned with my arguments for the ethical treatment of addicted persons and push for a rethinking of the place of the MDA in the United Kingdom's long-term strategy for the governance of people who consume drugs.

Over the course of recent decades, the over-emphasis on law and order as the prominent solution to the drug problem has been recognized to be essentially flawed (Barton, 2003). As such, it has paved the way for harm reduction strategies to play a larger role in effecting real policy changes. The realities of drugs and drug consumption practices in the 21st century have demanded such a change, late as it may be in catching up. Many authors began to take notice of the fact that the drug landscape was markedly different from the one only a decade ago (Parker et al., 1998). Recreational drug use became an inextricable component of most leisure activities, which in turn normalized drug use in the larger culture (Aldridge et al., 1999).

Such a normalization, of course, goes against the entire ethos of the "War on Drugs" and provided a clear antithetical position to the rhetoric used within the efforts of the war on drugs regarding the perceived dangers of psychoactive substances. This clash was precisely what exacerbated the broader acceptance of recreational drugs and the normalization of their use as leisure components among young people: the subjective experience of a dissociated inculcated discourse from the actual experience of drug consumption (MacCoun & Reuter, 2001). Such lived realities, along with the comparative view of other countries adopting a decriminalization approach, and by all accounts finding great success in most metrics of social wellbeing after the fact (Van Het Loo et al., 2002; Blackman, 2004)), are what have propelled the discourse on harm reduction strategies as the better alternative to deal with drug-related harm in UK drug policy. Indeed, the United Kingdom has followed suit on the general decrease of punishment measures of other European countries, incremental and slow though those decreases may be, such as the reclassification of cannabis from a class B to a class C substance. And such changes have somewhat informally rendered the cultural stigmatization towards cannabis usage less severe (Monaghan, 2011).

It would be a mistake, however, to believe that this "normalization" constitutes a true paradigmatic shift in terms of the underlying philosophy driving policymaking as it pertains to drug use and addiction. Understanding the international context, and the comparative lens through which the United Kingdom can be measured against more permissive societies, helps to visualize certain metrics and data (e.g., sanctions, incarceration rates, overdose deaths, etc.), but doesn't truly reveal the structural and historical differences that have informed the political discourse in the United Kingdom. The underlying motivation behind policymaking will inform the type of evidence and information that is cited in "evidence-based policy".

Referring back to Robin Room's conception of the constructionist model of the drug problem, it is worth noting how the predominant disciplinary view of a phenomenon will inform the problematization and therefore the policy constructs aimed at dealing with said phenomenon. In the case of drug consumption and addiction, a sociological view of the problem will inform the efforts to contain and minimize the "socially deviant" practice of hard drug consumption, such as is the case of the Netherlands. A more psychiatric-leaning view will inform the medico-legal approach towards the treatment of drug over-consumption as a problem to be dealt with within the purview of clinicians. Ideally, an epidemiologically- and-neurobiologically-based approach within the United Kingdom would lean towards the type of public health policy measures advocated for by harm reduction strategists in terms of substantive policy change.

But if the stated aim of UK drug policy, through the distinct phases and iterations of legislative reform, is that of reducing the prevalence of use of the substances in question, then by all metrics and accounts these laws have not succeeded in their goal. In the past decade, the United Kingdom has consistently had some of the highest rates of illicit drug use in Europe, with over 10 million people in England and Wales estimated to have used illicit drugs at least once (Roe, 2005).

The hypothesis of this chapter, and a key element of the argument of my book, is that this failure of UK drug policy to reduce the prevalence of illicit drug use has at least in part been due to its failure to mobilize an evidence-based, scientifically up-to-date, comprehensive understanding of addicted persons' condition and their compromised level of agency. This failure is then at the root of the exacerbated harms that can be related to drug use, which can include overdose deaths, unsafe sharing of injection needles leading to the spreading of infectious diseases, and poor social conditions due to stigmatization of drug abuse (e.g., less employment opportunities, etc.). The bioethical argument of my book goes hand in hand with the hypothesis that an evidence-based understanding of the compromised agency of addicted persons would reduce such harms more effectively: it would be a more ethical treatment of persons suffering from a disorder largely beyond their realm of control, autonomy, and thus responsibility.

Account of Agency in Criminal Responsibility

> In essence, then, politicised areas are adversarial domains, located at the crossroads of autonomous department boundaries. Holistically – particularly in the UK – drug policy lies at the interface between public health and criminal justice. It is not unique in spanning different policy precincts. Indeed, UK penal policies and those from elsewhere have flirted with both social welfare impulses of rehabilitation and more criminal justice-oriented goals of discipline and control.
>
> (Monaghan, 2011, p.43)

In the United Kingdom, a vast majority of persons incarcerated are found to be under the influence of a mind-altering substance at the moment of arrest, and many people arrested for drug-related crimes (e.g., possession, trafficking, sale, etc.) are found to be addicted to the substance in question once they are monitored in the prison setting (Zhang, 2003). A study looking at the health inequalities among people in contact with the criminal justice system found that 72% of male, and 71% of female prisoners were found to suffer from two or more mental disorders (including personality disorder, psychosis, neurosis, alcohol misuse and drug dependence) (RDA, 2013). In a subsequent study of offenders on probation, 72% of those identified as having a mental illness were also found to have a substance misuse problem.

With such a large overlap between criminality and drug use, the attitude that our legal system takes towards addicted persons is of vital importance, not only from a cost-effective point of view, considering the treatment and rehabilitation for convicted criminals in the custody of the State, but also from an ethical standpoint, seeing as the conviction and sentencing of many of these crimes is largely influenced by the illicit nature of the substance in question. Herein lies the problem of criminalizing substance abuse in a way that seems to punish the very phenomenon of being addicted. Speaking only of the ontological reality of being addicted as a mental and physical condition, it is important to note that *being addicted* is not a crime. Yet, the simple possession and consumption of an illicit substance, both necessary precedents to becoming addicted to the substance in the first place, are indeed criminal acts. I make the distinction only to highlight the inherent disconnect between the impossibility and unjustifiability of a mental state being legally sanctioned, and the inextricably correlated action actually being a crime.

Clearly distinguishing between the moral and legal responsibility of people who happen to be addicted to an illicit substance becomes a complicated issue. Indeed many of the criminal acts often associated with drug use are punished by law (e.g., theft, aggravated assault, etc.), but there is not an inevitable correlation of criminality with substance abuse among all addicted persons. This is significant if we want to maintain the normative claim that being addicted ought to be treated as a medical condition, i.e. suffering from a brain disease, instead of a criminal behaviour.

Inherent to legal conceptions of the responsibility of addicted persons is then the explanatory model one chooses to apply to the phenomenon of addictive behaviour, especially if one accepts that such behaviour is the root cause of the ensuing criminal activity. The very advances in neuroscience that are used to put forth a brain disease model of addiction can equally contribute to confusing ways of thinking about the criminal responsibility of addicted persons, i.e. an image of a literal impossibility of acting otherwise. "*Even sophisticated people tend to think that the 'man with the golden arm' is somehow an automaton, a puppet pulled by the narcotic strings of a biological disease, and that therefore the addict is not responsible for actions associated with his addiction*" (Morse, 2009).

This view is in sharp contrast to the opposing school of thought which attributes moral weakness to all actions associated with addiction, criminal or otherwise. And it is worth noting that these various characterizations, regardless of their truth value in accurately describing what happens inside a person's mind when they are under the influence of psychoactive substances, have great persuasive power. Regardless of what explanatory model we may choose for why addicted persons continue engaging in addictive behaviour, neuroreductionist or moralised, when it comes to their dealings with criminal law, the question is: how should their status as addicted persons affect their liability for criminal behaviour (related to their addiction), if it should at all?

Hopefully, this line of inquiry shows why it was important to establish an account of agency in the first chapters of this book, and then provide a neuroscientific explanation of why an addicted person's agency might be compromised whilst in the throes of addiction. The debate might very well continue as to the degree to which addicted persons may exert control over their actions and their continued substance use. Indeed, if we adhere to the brain disease model of addiction (BDMA), then any action related to their addiction would be but a manifestation of said brain disease, a symptom of the underlying pathology. On the other hand, if we adhere to the moral weakness view, then criminal liability rests solely on the person who continues to seek and use drugs, regardless of how constrained their subsequent choices might be.

Despite the empirical evidence for the BDMA and the continuing research which shows the extent of the mitigating factors that might compromise an addicted person's agency, I will argue in the following segment that criminal law in the United Kingdom maintains the position that addiction-related actions remain within the control of the person committing them and are thus consistent with traditional justifications for criminal responsibility and thus punishment. Working through the general principles at play in the criminal justice system's attitude towards addicted persons (intention, compulsive behaviour, mitigating excuses for irrational actions, etc.), it is possible to have a general idea of the legal perspective towards addiction-related criminal behaviour and the inherent flaws within the system's consideration and subsequent treatment of addicted persons.

The BDMA and Moral Responsibility in Cases of Addiction

The question of moral responsibility in addiction is obviously affected by the Brain Disease Model of Addiction and the lingering question of whether to conceive of it as either a disease or a choice. This duality shapes not only legal and ethical considerations but also the societal response to those struggling with addiction. This question touches on fundamental issues about human agency, self-control, and the conditions under which individuals can be held accountable for their actions.

If addicted persons are seen as suffering from a brain disease, then their moral responsibility ought naturally to be slightly mitigated. This perspective aligns with the medical view that suggests that addiction is a chronic condition characterized by compulsive drug seeking and use, despite harmful consequences. Some authors argue that addiction impairs the very capacities that are central to moral responsibility, such as rational decision-making and self-control (Levy, 2013). From this point of view, addicted persons are seen as patients rather than wilful criminals. The BDMA promotes the idea that addiction is not a failure of will but a consequence of neurobiological factors that reduce an individual's capacity to weigh and choose their actions freely.

This perspective has profound implications for society's policy response, of course. If addiction is a disease, then the addicted person's actions are seen as symptoms of their condition rather than voluntary choices. Society may, therefore, adopt a more compassionate and rehabilitative approach, emphasizing treatment over punishment. For instance, drug courts and rehabilitation programs may be seen as preferable to incarceration, recognizing that the root cause of the behaviour is a neurobiological issue rather than a moral failing. The concept of diminished responsibility, which I will delve into later on in this chapter, comes into play, where the addict's culpability is lessened due to their impaired capacity for self-control.

However, viewing addiction purely as a disease can also be counter-productive. Some critics may argue that this approach risks absolving individuals of personal responsibility entirely, leading to a paternalistic view where addicted persons are seen as incapable of making any rational choices. Indeed, many thinkers caution against a simplistic application of the disease model, noting that it could undermine the agency of individuals, suggesting they are merely victims of their neurobiology. This can have unintended consequences, such as reducing the motivation for recovery if addicts believe they have no control over their behaviour, a sort of self-fulfilling prophecy of determinism which has been empirically observed in some cases (Dotsenko & Pchelina, 2021).

On the other hand, when addiction is framed as a choice, the narrative shifts towards holding individuals fully accountable for their actions. This perspective sees addiction as a result of poor choices or a lack of willpower. Here, moral responsibility is emphasized, and addicted persons are viewed as individuals who have made poor decisions, despite knowing the harmful consequences of their choices. The societal response, in this case, often leans towards punitive measures, such as criminalization and stigmatization, under the belief that addicted persons should be held fully accountable for their actions.

The choice model, as is now apparent, oversimplifies the complex nature of addiction by ignoring the psychological, social, and biological factors that contribute to it. It fails to recognize that once addiction takes hold, the ability to choose freely is often severely compromised. Levy points out that the insistence on viewing addiction as a choice ignores the reality of how addiction changes the brain, making it difficult, if not impossible, for the individual to exercise self-control in the way that non-addicted persons do (Levy, 2013).

In reality, the policy response to the question of addicted persons' actions must lie somewhere between these two extremes. Acknowledging addiction as a disease does not necessarily negate the idea of personal responsibility, rather it contextualizes the situation. It suggests that while addicted persons may be responsible for seeking help and working towards recovery, their capacity for making rational decisions is impaired, and they may require support and treatment to regain control over their lives. This balanced view would promote a more compassionate yet responsible approach, where society recognizes the complexity of addiction without stripping individuals of their agency. In terms of the actual legal frameworks that should be put in place to take into account this sense of compromised agency, the question remains somewhat nebulous still. However, we can look at some examples of instances where criminal liability is mitigated due to special circumstances, and ask whether that perspective can be applied to the case of addicted persons.

Mitigating Factors for Compromised Agency in Criminal Law

> *...terming addiction a disease and characterizing seeking and using as signs does not answer the question of moral and legal responsibility.*
>
> (Morse, 2019, p.541)

In Stephen J. Morse's view of the relationship between criminal law and addiction, there is a presupposition of a "*folk psychological*" view of a person and their behaviour as understood through the lens of desires, beliefs, intentions, volitions, and plans (Morse, 2009). In other words, the criminal justice system does not operate in complex and deconstructed understandings of what may impair a person's ability to form such mental states, it satisfies itself in accepting that a person will have those mental states and is preoccupied rather with clearly defining and categorizing those mental states according to their consequence on a person's actions. Morse acknowledges that a bioethical debate can take place between legal, scientific, and philosophical conceptions of those mental states and their impact on a theory of human action, but this debate cannot undermine the claim that mental states are the foundation of criminal legal theory.

> Folk psychology does not presuppose the truth of free will, [...] does not hold that we have minds that are independent of our bodies [...], and it presupposes no particular moral or political view. It does not claim that all mental states are conscious or that people go through a conscious decision-making process each time that they act. It allows for "thoughtless," automatic, and habitual actions and for non-conscious intentions. [...] The definition insists only that human action is in part causally explained by mental states.
>
> (Morse, 2019, p. 542)

As Morse goes on to explain, one of the fundamental pillars of criminal law is the fact that the criteria necessary for criminal responsibility are actions accompanied by relevant mental states or mens rea, for example the act of killing with the accompanying intention to kill being the prerequisites for homicide. This basic principle of jurisprudence concerns the place of agency in criminal law, and as such Morse compares this with the criteria for addictive behaviour, saying "*The criminal law's criteria for responsibility, like the criteria for addiction, are acts and mental states*"

(Morse, 2019, p.542). However, this is precisely the conflation at the heart of the criminal law's approach to drug-related crimes that I aim to unpack and revise.

If one adheres to a view of addiction as an exhibit of irrational behaviour, in which the addicted person has made sub-optimal choices and engages in addictive behaviour as a result, then Morse's notion that addiction is characterized by poor impulse control indeed should not mitigate their criminal responsibility. But the tenet of the BDMA is precisely that there is no formal intention on the part of the addicted person to engage in the behaviour, it is a compulsive action akin to other actions wherein the underlying intention is absent. Morse uses some of these examples and provides a view according to which the criminal law would acknowledge that an affirmative legal defense could be mounted which would negate responsibility even if those elements of a mental state had been established.

> Excuses exist when the defendant has done wrong but is not responsible for his behavior. Using general descriptive language, the excusing conditions are lack of reasonable capacity for acting rationally and lack of reasonable capacity for self-control (although the latter is more controversial than the former). The so-called cognitive and control tests for legal insanity are examples of these excusing conditions.
>
> (Morse, 2019, p. 543)

These excusing conditions include cases which aim to assess the culpability of an individual invoking a plea of insanity. In these cases, the opinion of forensic mental health clinicians is more and more called upon to assess the mental state of the defendant. Some authors have reviewed the literature and pertinent case law for the concept of "settled insanity", which aims to discuss the potential for a threshold condition for forensic clinicians evaluating the viability of an insanity defense when it is invoked (Feix & Wolber, 2007).

Recent research on the effects of long-term substance abuse provides an opportunity to revise the analogy between insanity pleas and cases of addiction-related compromised agency. This view can today benefit from ever-more detailed psychiatric forensic evidence, which allows for the courts to assess the impairment of a person's mental state, to consider that mental health issues can often be correlated with substance abuse disorders to a significant degree (Monaghan, 2011), and thus to provide a fair and humane consideration of the legal culpability of a person (Chandler et al., 2009), taking into consideration how substance abuse can lead to a permanent state of impaired cognition and/or volition.

A concrete example of what this might look like is the M'Naghten Rule, which is a metric used to assess the successful plea of insanity invoked when an individual convicted of a crime has a "defect of reason, from disease of the mind" (M'Naghten case, 1843) and thus could not understand the moral nature of their actions. This case occurred in the United Kingdom, when Daniel M'Naghten unsuccessfully attempted to assassinate the British Prime Minister, shooting his secretary instead, who died a few days later. M'Naghten was charged with murder but acquitted on the grounds that he was insane. The acquittal caused some controversy, so the House of Lords asked a panel of judges to review the law governing insanity and the two following rules arose:

1 "every defendant is presumed sane unless the contrary is proved;"
2 "to successfully plead insanity, it must be clearly proved that at the time of committing the act the defendant was labouring under such a defect of reason, from disease of the mind, so as not to know the nature and quality of the act they were doing; or, if they did know it, that they did not know what they were doing was wrong."

(UKHL, 1843)

In accordance with this rule, the source of whatever affected mental state causes the individual to break the law then has to be demonstrable in court (e.g., a mental state stemming from a pre-existing psychiatric condition or induced by stressful events), and following this demonstration, under section 5 of the Criminal Procedure (Insanity) Act of 1964:

the sentence for the offence to which the finding relates is fixed by law (e.g. murder), the court must make a hospital order (see section 37 Mental Health Act 1983) with a restriction order limiting discharge and other rights (see section 41 Mental Health Act 1983).

In any other case the court may make:

- a hospital order (with or without a restriction order);
- a supervision order; or
- an order for absolute discharge.

This is of course a much more desirable outcome than incarceration. Therefore, if a similar rule were to be established in the case of drug-related crime, the conceptual difficulty would lie in distinguishing between:

- an acute intoxication/alteration of the mental state of the defendant through substance consumption at a specific point in time;
  and
- the persistent nature of a mental disorder characterized by compulsive behaviour over long periods of time, punctuated by moments of consumption.

In certain jurisdictions, the test for finding an accused defendant legally insane necessitates either a lack of understanding that their actions were wrong (cognitive impairment) and/or a lack of ability to refrain themselves from doing that which they knew was wrong (volitional impairment). This came about in the 1960s, when the American Law Institute developed its Model Penal Code to include a recommendation for a test for insanity that would include both cognitive and volitional parts (ALI, 1985). One example of the impact of such legislative reform is a comprehensive review of the in-depth clinical evaluation of 1,446 defendants presenting a legal insanity plea in Maryland state, USA (Donohue et al., 2008) and its findings which show a significant percentage of those having secured a successful legal insanity court decision being found non-criminally responsible (NCR) due to volitional impairment alone (around 11% of the 416 defendants found NCR). The factors considered by forensic psychiatric evaluators included psychiatric symptoms and underlying markers for mental illnesses.

One ethical consideration of an attempt to establish an analogical "addiction/insanity" defense would be that a person, by invoking the fact that they were legally insane when under the influence of mind-altering drugs, would be refuting the conceptualization that sees drug users as independent and free agents, a view that some public health efforts champion.

Certain legal jurisdictions do distinguish "*between mental impairment that does not go beyond the period of voluntary intoxication, for which no defense is available, and insanity resulting from long-term use of drugs or alcohol*" (Slovenko, 2003, p. 269) and

> a majority of jurisdictions in the United States have recognized a defense to criminal acts where long-term, voluntary use of an intoxicant has caused a fixed or 'settled insanity' that is distinct from and independent of the period of intoxication
>
> (Carter-Yamauchi, 1998, p. 48)

Interpretations of this possible distinction are at the discretion of the courts, of course, and such interpretations can range from the dismissal of an insanity defense outright due to the intoxication being considered a voluntary act committed by the individual, to the allowance of a defense when such voluntary intoxication is considered to be a temporary exacerbation of an already existing psychosis. These different court decisions can then have a real impact on the discourse concerning the BDMA and its relevance as a conceptualization of addiction, since the conclusions presented can offer very condemning views on the disease model of addiction and further dispel the notion that it can have any basis as a causal explanation of behaviour:

The Senate Judiciary Committee, in discussion of the Act, stated that, "the voluntary use of alcohol or drugs, even if they render the defendant unable to appreciate the nature and quality of his acts, does not constitute insanity" [...] The courts have generally not upheld substance-induced psychotic symptoms as providing for an insanity defense when the substance in question had been taken voluntarily. In the murder case of Downing v. Commonwealth, the defense attempted to make the case that the defendant had become "uncharacteristically aggressive" and later had amnesia for the event due to a "grossly altered state" as a result of intoxication. The court ruled

> drunkenness [voluntary] may have even produced temporary insanity during the instance when a crime was committed, and yet it would afford no excuse [...] ... the term involuntary intoxication (particularly as it relates to a disease model of addiction) is a "confusing pseudo-simplification" and "would be a grave error"; that is, the disease model can imply that the subject has no control over consumption and is therefore not responsible for addiction-related behavior.
>
> (Feix & Wolber, 2007)

This concept of "settled insanity" would then present a challenge in the criminal law's conception of drug-related crime and the ethical and legal standards for making such a distinction are far more complicated. This plea of "addiction/insanity" would need to put forth the argument that said insanity came about from a literal inability to exert control over cravings, and that something akin to a compulsion had taken hold of the defendant. The problem is that under various commonly understood notions of the concept of compulsion, the case of addicted persons' exhibited lack of self-control when it comes to their habit does not qualify as a compelled action (Heather, 2017).

However, there is the possibility of reworking the concept of compulsion, so that addicted persons' impulse control difficulties may be regarded as compulsive in such a way that might provide the mitigation necessary for a criminological conceptualization of an addicted person's responsibility. In his chapter, "Addiction and Compulsion", Neil Levy mobilizes the notion of "ego-depletion" (Levy, 2010a) in order to conciliate the concept of a compulsive act in the context of addiction: on the one hand, it is very much a matter of the ego's ability to control urges, hence a matter of personal choice; on the other hand, it is definitely an observable phenomenon that the resource in question is being depleted, and hence an observable "relapsing disease".

Indeed, whereas in other instances the focus may be on the strength of the craving per se or in the effect that a particular substance will have on the brain's neural mechanisms, in looking at ego depletion, Levy shifts the focus towards the mind itself and its capacity to resist any urge, not just the particularly strong urges brought about by addictive substances. Forget resisting heroin, this particular concept looks at what makes a chocolate chip cookie irresistible under certain circumstances. The argument from ego depletion and the variability of the concept of compulsion is that irresistibility ought to be relativized depending on the agent in question, not necessarily depending on the substance in question.

> *...a desire is not irresistible in itself, but irresistible to a given agent at a given time.*
>
> (Neil Levy, 2010b, p. 271)

Of course, the moment the urge arises is not the only point at which this notion of ego depletion will come into play. As has been mentioned in previous chapters, the entire environment and set of circumstances leading up to the moment of consumption are replete with individual moments of choice where the irresistibility of the urge to engage in a certain action is as crucial as the actual moment of substance consumption (e.g., think of the moment a person stares at the car keys deciding whether or not to drive to the liquor store, this moment being just as ego-depleting as the moment the person takes a sip of alcohol). There is sufficient evidence to show that minute and seemingly innocuous actions leading up to the consumption of a drug can take on equally automatic and irresistible characteristics (West, 2006).

Conceiving the change in the motivational set of circumstances as being the main element responsible for an agent being able to resist an urge, this notion could then be extrapolated into a criminal law perspective where the focus of policies could shift from looking at substances and/or motivational factors linked with drug consumption, and instead look at the possibility of changing a motivational set of circumstances within the environment that an addicted person will find themselves in, therefore providing the necessary mitigating factors that Morse alludes to in mentioning cognitive and control tests used for legal insanity defenses. A comprehensive comparative review of the neuroscientific basis for the legal defense of cognitive impairment in insanity and cognitive impairment in addiction is beyond the scope of this chapter, but this analogical comparison provides sufficient cause to critically analyze why a strategy for more effective policy-making with regard to drug-related harms has not been established through a basis of neuroscientific research on the compromised agency of addicted persons and as such their mitigated level of criminal responsibility.

This type of policy-making strategy would then pave the way for the focus of addiction policies to turn towards providing treatment options, knowledge, and social resources to make sure that their cravings do not last too long or occur too often, so as to not overwhelm their capacity for self-control and thus be able to replenish their measure of self-control and have a chance at recovery. The distinction between these types of policy frameworks will be the focus of the next and final chapter.

Conclusion

In this chapter, I have reviewed a narrative of UK drug policy as a series of milestone legislative events marked by an evolving conceptualization of addiction. This conceptualization of addiction has revolved around the notion of agency and the basis for the criminal law's account of responsibility. I have attempted to unpack that conceptualization, as well as provide the foundation for potential mitigation in the case of addicted persons' responsibility if they were to be considered to "be suffering from" addiction, instead of "choosing to be" addicted.

In 1998, after UN member states declared the goal of a "drug-free world", the UN General Assembly Special Session on the World Drug Problem estimated that 8 million people in the world used heroin, about 13 million used cocaine, 30 million used amphetamine-type substances (ATS), and over 135 million consumed cannabis. Ten years later, the UN estimated that 12 million people used heroin, 16 million used cocaine, almost 34 million used ATS, and over 165 million used cannabis. The worldwide area under opium poppy cultivation was estimated at about 238,000 hectares in 1998, and in 2008 was 235,700 hectares, which did represent a small decline. From this ten-year comparative review, it became clear that the strategy of prohibitionist measures aimed at eradicating the world of its addiction problem had not been effective (Csete et al., 2016).

In the next chapter, I will attempt to provide an argument as to why this geopolitical strategy has not been effective, based on the conceptual groundwork that I have laid out throughout the previous chapters. Furthermore, I will argue that the goals of "effectiveness in reducing societal harms of addiction" and "ethical treatment of addicted persons" go hand in hand when it comes to constructing policy strategies. This argument will rely on the premise that a harm reduction strategy is conceived of with the objective of providing humane treatment for what is considered a medical disorder, and as such is more effective in reducing the harms associated with drug abuse. I will present cases that show a distinction in the conceptualization of addiction, and present the results which show a clearly more effective method of policy construction, as well as arguments for the types of reforms that would implement such policy constructs into a national effort to treat addicted persons more ethically.

Note

1 A thorough review of the alternative conceptions of addiction as either an irrational or immoral choice, of which there are plenty, is beyond the scope of this chapter. For the sake of an analogical dichotomy between the two different types of policy constructs I will discuss in the following chapter, I will simply divide the philosophical conceptions of addiction in policy-making discussions as either embracing the view that addiction is a brain disease and thus ought to be primarily treated as a medical condition, and those which do not accept such a view.

References

Aldridge, J., Parker, H., & Measham, F. (1999). *Drug Trying And Drug Use Across Adolescence: A Longitudinal Study Of Young People's Drug Taking In Two Regions of Northern England*. DPAS Paper 1. London: Drugs Prevention Advisory Service.

ALI Model Penal Code, § 4.01. 1985.

Barton, A. (2003). *Illicit Drugs: Use and Control*. London: Routledge.

Bennett, T., & Holloway, K. (2005). *Understanding Drugs, Alcohol And Crime*. Buckingham: Open University Press.

Berridge, V. (1984). Drugs and Social Policy: The Establishment of Drug Control in Britain 1900–1930. *British Journal of Addiction*, *79*, 17–29.

Blackman, S. (2004). *Chilling Out: The Cultural Politics of Substance Consumption, Youth and Drug Policy*. Buckingham: Open University Press.

Carter-Yamauchi, C.A. (1998). *Drugs, Alcohol, and the Insanity Defense: The Debate Over "settled" Insanity*. Legislative Reference Bureau.

Chandler, R.K., Fletcher, B.W., & Volkow, N.D. (2009). Treating Drug Abuse and Addiction in the Criminal Justice System: Improving Public Health and Safety. *JAMA*, *301*(2), 183–190. https://doi.org/10.1001/jama.2008.976

Csete, J., et al. (2016). Public Health and International Drug Policy. *Lancet (London, England)*, *387*(10026), 1427–1480.

Donohue, A., Arya, V., Fitch, L., & Hammen, D. (2008). Legal Insanity. *Psychiatry (Edgmont)*, *5*(3), 58–66.

Dotsenko, E.L., & Pchelina, O.V. (2021). Free Will as a Paradox: Empirical Evaluation of the Construct of Everyday Consciousness. *Psychology in Russia: State of the Art*, *14*(2), 137–151. https://doi.org/10.11621/pir2021.0109

EMCDDA. (2019). United Kingdom Country Drug Report 2019. [online] *EMCDDA*. Available at: https://www.emcdda.europa.eu/countries/drug-reports/2019/united-kingdom_en

Heather, N. (2017). Is the concept of compulsion useful in the explanation or description of addictive behaviour and experience? *Addictive Behaviors Reports*, *6*, 15–38. https://doi.org/10.1016/j.abrep.2017.05.002

Hellman, M. (2021). Understanding Addiction: The Shift from Epistemology to Ontology. *Behavioural Brain Research*, *412*, 113416.

Holland, A. (2020). An Ethical Analysis of UK Drug Policy as an Example of A Criminal Justice Approach To Drugs: A Commentary on the Short Film Putting UK Drug Policy into Focus. *Harm Reduction Journal*, *17*(1), 97. https://doi.org/10.1186/s12954-020-00434-8

Kohn, M. (2001). *Dope Girls: The Birth of the British Drug Underground*. London: Granta Books.

Levy, N. (2010a). Addiction and Compulsion. In *A Companion to the Philosophy of Action* (pp. 267–273). John Wiley & Sons, Ltd. https://doi.org/10.1002/9781444323528.ch34

M'Naghten's case [1843] UKHL J16 (19 June 1843). http://www.bailii.org/uk/cases/UKHL/1843/J16.html; Citation: (1843) 10 Cl & F 200, 1 Car & Kir 130, [1843] UKHL J16, [1843-60] All ER 229, 10 Cl & F 200, 8 ER 718

MacCoun, R., & Reuter, P. (2001). Evaluating Alternative Cannabis Regimes. *The British Journal of Psychiatry*, *178*, 123–128.

Monaghan, M. (2011). *Evidence Versus Politics: Exploiting Research in UK drug policy making?* The Policy Press, University of Bristol.

Morse, S.J. (2009). Addiction, Science, and Criminal Responsibility. In N.A. Farahany (Ed.), *The Impact of Behavioral Sciences on Criminal Law* (pp. 241–288). Oxford University Press. https://doi.org/10.1093/acprof:oso/9780195340525.003.0008

Morse, S.J. (2019). Criminal Law and Addiction. In Hanna Pickard and Serge H. Ahmed (Eds.), *The Routledge Handbook of Philosophy and Science of Addiction* (pp. 540–553). U of Penn Law School, Public Law Research Paper No. 18–35. https://ssrn.com/abstract=3271890

Parker, H., Aldridge, J., & Measham, F. (1998). *Illegal Leisure: The Normalization Adolescent of Recreational Drug Use.* London: Routledge.

Reuter, P., & Stevens, A. (2007). *An Analysis of UK Drug Policy.*

Roe, S. (2005). Drug Misuse Declared: Findings from the 2005/06 British Crime Survey. In *Home Office Statistical Bulletin 16/05.* London: Home Office.

Seddon, T. (2009). *A History of Drugs: Drugs and Freedom in the Liberal Age.* Taylor & Francis.

Seddon, T., Ralphs, R., & Williams, L. (2008). Risk, Security and the "criminalization" of British Drug Policy. *British Journal of Criminology, 48*(4), 818–34.

Slovenko, R. (2003). The Insanity Defense: Matricide in a French Quarter Hotel. *The Journal of Psychiatry & Law, 31*(2), 251–283.

South, N. (1997). Drugs: Use, Crime And Control. In M. Maguire, R. Morgan and R. Reiner (Eds.), *The Oxford Handbook of Criminology* (pp. 925–960). Oxford: Oxford University Press.

Spear, H.B., & Mott, J. (1993). Cocaine and Crack within the "British system": A History of Control. In P. Bean (Ed.), Cocaine and Crack: Supply and Use. London: The Macmillan Press.

Stevens, A. (2007). When Two Dark Figures Collide: Evidence And Discourse On Drug Related Crime. *Critical Social Policy, 27*(1), 77–99.

Stimson, G., & Lart, R. (1994). The Relationship Between State And Local Practice In The Development Of A National Policy On Drugs Between 1920–1990. In J. Strang and M. Gossop (Eds.), *Heroin Addiction And Drug Policy: The British System* (pp. 331–341). Oxford: Oxford University Press.

Strang, J., & Gossop, M. (1994). The British System: Visionary Anticipation or Masterly Inactivity. In J. Strang and M. Gossop (Eds.), *Heroin Addiction and Drug Policy: The British System* (pp. 342–351). Oxford: Oxford University Press.

Strang, J., & Sheridan, J. (2006). Heroin and Methadone Prescriptions From A London Drug Clinic Over The First 15 Years Of Operation (1968–1983): Old Records Examined. *Substance Use & Misuse, 41*(9), 1227–1238.

United Nations High Commissioner for Human Rights. (2015). *Study on the Impact of the World Drug Problem on the Enjoyment Of Human Rights.* Human Rights Council, 30th session.

Van Het Loo, M., Van Beusekom, I., & Kahan, J.P. (2002). Decriminalization of Drug Use In Portugal: The Development Of A Policy. *Annals of the American Academy of Political Science, 582*(1), 49–63.

Zhang, Z. (2003). *Drug And Alcohol Use And Related Matters Among Arrestees.* National Opinion Research Center, ADAM.

West, R. (2006). *Theory of Addiction*. Blackwells.
Levy, N. (2010b). Addiction and compulsion. In T. O'Connor & C. Sandis (Eds.), *A Companion to the Philosophy of Action* (pp. 267–273). Wiley-Blackwell.
Feix, J., & Wolber, G. (2007). Intoxication and settled insanity: a finding of not guilty by reason of insanity. *The Journal of the American Academy of Psychiatry and the Law*, *35*(2), 172–182.
Levy, N. (Ed.). (2013). *Addiction and Self-Control: Perspectives from Philosophy, Psychology, and Neuroscience*. Oxford University Press.
Buchman, D.Z., Skinner, W., & Illes, J. (2010). Negotiating the relationship between addiction, ethics, and brain science. *AJOB Neuroscience*, *1*(1), 36–45.
Heather, N., & Segal, G. (2013). Understanding addiction: Donald Davidson and the problem of akrasia. *Addiction Research & Theory*, *21*(6), 445–452. https://doi.org/10.3109/16066359.2012.754014
Room, R. (2006). Addiction concepts and international control. *The Social History of Alcohol and Drugs*, *21*(2), 276–289.
Guerra-Doce, E. (2015). Psychoactive substances in prehistoric times: examining the archaeological evidence. *Time and Mind*, *8*(1), 91–112. https://doi.org/10.1080/1751696X.2014.993244
Stevens, A. (2011). *Drugs, crime and public health: The political economy of drug policy*. Routledge.
Revolving Doors Agency. (2013). *Balancing act: Addressing health inequalities among people in contact with the criminal justice system*. Revolving Doors Agency.

Chapter 5

Harm Reduction Strategies

Implementations and Challenges

Introduction

Harm reduction has emerged in recent decades as an approach that seeks not to remove harmful practices (sometimes referred to as "vices") from society, but rather to minimize the negative impacts that these may have, attenuating the health, social, and environmental impacts that are associated with these harmful practices, without requiring or preaching abstinence from the practitioners of these "vices".

Far from the punitive ideology motivating prohibitionist policies, it is more of a pragmatic strategy, designed to offer support and resources that reduce the harms associated with high-risk behaviours. However, while the intentions of harm reduction strategies such as safe injection sites and drug decriminalization aim to improve public health outcomes, they also raise some ethical dilemmas. These revolve around the tension between achieving public health goals and respecting the individual autonomy of persons engaging in these high-risk behaviours.

The ethical foundations of harm reduction are rooted in principles of humanism and a pragmatic approach to public health. In their work, "Harm Reduction: Pragmatic Strategies for Managing High-Risk Behaviors", G. Alan Marlatt, Mary E. Larimer and Katie Witkiewitz provide a comprehensive examination of harm reduction as a public health strategy aimed at minimizing the negative consequences of high-risk behaviours, particularly psychoactive substance abuse. The book offers a practical and theoretical framework for understanding and implementing harm reduction strategies, emphasizing the importance of meeting individuals "where they are" rather than insisting on abstinence. It explores various approaches, including needle exchange programs and safe injection sites, while discussing the ethical, social, and policy implications of these strategies.

According to these authors, harm reduction prioritizes reducing the adverse consequences of drug use over eliminating the behaviour itself. Once again, this approach is fundamentally a pragmatic one, recognizing that while some individuals may not be ready or able to abstain from

DOI: 10.4324/9781003582908-6

drug use, our society can still take steps to protect their health and wellbeing.

At the same time, Marlatt et al. insist that harm reduction is grounded in humanism, emphasizing the dignity and rights of individuals who use drugs. This perspective challenges the moralistic and punitive approaches that have historically dominated drug policy, advocating instead for compassionate and evidence-based interventions that respect individual autonomy.

Safe injection sites, for example, provide a controlled environment where individuals can inject drugs under the supervision of trained health professionals. These facilities have become the archetypical harm reduction project in our collective consciousness, as they aim to reduce the risks associated with drug use, such as overdose, the spread of infectious diseases, and unsafe injection practices, by providing a sterile and medically safe environment where addicted persons may inject themselves with whatever substance they are currently using. Studies have shown that these sites can significantly reduce harm to individuals and communities, contributing to lower rates of overdose deaths and the transmission of diseases like HIV and Hepatitis C (Marlatt et al., 2011).

However, implementing safe injection sites also raises some ethical concerns. One of the primary criticisms levied against this type of project is the possible perception that these sites may condone or even encourage drug use. Critics argue that by providing a safe space for drug use, society may be implicitly endorsing the behaviour, potentially undermining efforts to discourage drug use overall. This concern highlights a broader ethical tension: the need to balance harm reduction with the societal interest of drug use prevention.

Furthermore, safe injection sites raise questions about autonomy and consent. While these sites are designed to empower individuals by providing safer options for drug use, they also operate within a context where the user's autonomy may be compromised. As we have seen in previous chapters, substance abuse disorders may impair judgement and decision-making capabilities, leading some to question whether individuals can be said to be exercising their full agential capacity when using these services.

Another arm of the harm reduction strategy is policy-based, aiming to reduce the negative consequences of drug use by eliminating criminal penalties for possession of small amounts of drugs. Instead of incarceration, individuals can be offered health interventions, such as counselling or treatment programs. The ethical rationale for decriminalization is based on the recognition that criminalizing drug use often exacerbates harm, leading to social marginalization, stigma, and further barriers to accessing the healthcare options necessary for cessation.

From a public health perspective, decriminalization can lead to significant improvements in health outcomes. One notable example that has often been cited is Portugal's decriminalization of drugs in 2001, which led to reductions in drug-related deaths, HIV infections, and drug-related crime. However, the ethical implications of decriminalization are complex. One key point of contention is the tension between protecting public health and maintaining public safety. Opponents of these decriminalization strategies in Portugal argued that it may have led to increased drug use and related harms, potentially jeopardizing community safety. These points will be further developed when looking at the different case studies of Canada and San Francisco in recent years.

Decriminalization also raises questions about justice and equity. While the strategy aims to reduce harms associated with drug use, it does not necessarily address the broader social determinants that contribute to drug use in the first place, such as poverty, inequality, and lack of access to education and healthcare. As a result, some critics also argue that decriminalization may perpetuate existing social injustices, particularly if it is not accompanied by broader efforts to address these underlying issues. Once again, if we are to critically analyze the reasons for the failed implementations of harm reduction strategies in cities like Vancouver and San Francisco, these are points often overlooked.

Finally, some ethical dilemmas associated with harm reduction ultimately revolve around the challenge of balancing public health goals with individual autonomy. Harm reduction strategies like safe injection sites and drug decriminalization prioritize the health and wellbeing of individuals, recognizing that punitive approaches to drug use often do more harm than good. However, these strategies also raise difficult questions about the role of the State in regulating individual behaviour and the extent to which society should intervene in the lives of individuals who use drugs, a point that more libertarian philosophies tend to oppose.

As we will hopefully see in this chapter, and especially in a continuation of the previous ones, one way to navigate these dilemmas is to adopt a nuanced understanding of autonomy that takes into account the social and psychological factors that influence decision-making. Rather than viewing autonomy as an all-or-nothing concept, it can be understood as a continuum, with varying degrees of autonomy depending on the individual's circumstances. This perspective allows for a more compassionate and context-sensitive approach to harm reduction, recognizing that individuals may require varying levels of support to make informed and autonomous decisions about their health. By critically examining all of these dilemmas and adopting a nuanced understanding of autonomy, policymakers and public health professionals can develop more ethical and effective approaches to harm reduction, improving the lives of people suffering from addiction and the communities in which they live.

Harm Reduction Strategies in the Narrative of Legislative Evolution of UK Drug Policy

The first objective, then, is to place harm reduction strategies as part of the narrative of legislative events in UK drug policy that was established in the previous chapter, in order to evaluate the ethical implications of said strategies. This chapter represents the culmination of the argument that I have constructed in the book, concerning the evolution of the conception of addiction among policy constructs. I have situated my conceptual analysis within a methodology of historical study intertwined with social policy analysis. This constitutes my contribution to the study of UK drug policy, i.e. the placement of "harm reduction" strategies as part of a historical narrative of legislative events that have sought, over the past few hundred years, to regulate and control the consumption of psychoactive substances in our modern, industrialized, and liberal societies (Berridge, 1999). Toby Seddon traces this historical narrative as a way of providing a critical perspective on the contemporary "drug problem". Beginning with the Pharmacy Act of 1868, Seddon's view is that the importance of this legislative event stems from the fact that it was the first time opium and opiate derivatives were seen as a *problem* that required a policy solution. While this conception of psychoactive substances as a particular problem for societies to need to tackle might seem commonplace today, this historical study aims precisely to dispel the notion that this was always the case, and shed light on the role that legislation has had in shaping societal views in the past couple of centuries. The Pharmacy Act of 1868 was also the beginning of the medico-legal nexus (Berridge, 1978a), wherein medical practitioners were seen as the appropriate gatekeepers for the provision of these problematic substances (opium and opium-based products), and as such has particular importance for current biopsychosocial conceptions of addiction as a medical, rather than criminal, problem (Skewes & Gonzalez, 2013). More than anything, this first legislative event in Seddon's narrative can be seen as the root of our current social and public health policy paradigmatic view, wherein the problem of drugs and drug users is one that needs to be tackled and can only be solved, via legislative regulation efforts.

Further on, the Dangerous Drugs Act of 1920 marks another important milestone in this chronology, establishing for the first time what appears to be self-evident in most views today, namely the fact that drugs like heroin and cocaine are a different category of psychoactive substances, and are in-and-of-themselves dangerous (unlike other substances and past conceptions, where the danger lay rather in the *abuse* of the substance), thus required to be controlled through a prohibitionist framework of criminal law. With the emergence of the modern Welfare State, the accompanying mentalities and social practices concerning the "public good" provide us with the necessary context to situate the Dangerous Drugs Act of 1920 as the consequent legislative event that would respond to the growing international need for a drug-control system (Berridge, 1978b). The transition to welfare liberalism at the turn of the 20th century ushered in the notion of state interventionism in the areas of social health (e.g., sobriety in public places), particularly with those who were seen as incapable of acting autonomously in their own best interest (i.e., inebriated people and/or addicted persons). As the starting point of the criminalization of these "dangerous" drugs, the legislative event that was the Dangerous Drugs Act of 1920 marks the beginning of one of the most important aspects of the current addiction problem: the debate on the criminalization of addiction.

Finally, jumping ahead to the most recent event in this legislative genealogy, the Drugs Act of 2005 marks the culmination of neoliberalist conceptions of risk management in the public sphere and the evolution of the governance conception of the drug problem to what is its most current form. Over the course of the second half of the 20th century, the idea shifted from "*the drugs represent a danger to the citizens*" into "*certain drug-users are dangerous to other citizens*". And herein lies the shift in policy conceptualization towards a drug strategy more concerned with risk-behaviour reduction (the seed of what we would now call "harm reduction" strategies) and the problematization of drug-users as seemingly rational and calculating agents, who should be encouraged to make responsible ("better") choices. In this last legislative event, we can see the final link between a world in which laudanum could be purchased along a bar of chocolate and the pint of milk for the week at the local pharmacy (1868), and the world we are in today, where illegal possession of valium can mean 5 years of prison time in the United Kingdom[1].

The objective of this summary of the genealogy of notable legislative events in the history of UK drug policy is important to set the stage for the type of policy I want to focus on: "harm reduction" strategies. In order to fully appreciate their deviation from what has come before, I choose to dedicate this section to the past policy frameworks in order to better understand the philosophical thesis of this chapter: that the effectiveness of a certain type of policy depends not on the soundness of the empirical data from which it is based (of which there was plenty in 1868, 1920, and 2005), nor from the political motivation behind its construction (questionable though they may be at any point in history). Rather, as Seddon demonstrates in his analysis of past policy frameworks, and as I hope to demonstrate in my distinction of current policy constructs, the effectiveness of a certain type of policy aimed at regulating and controlling the *problem* of addiction comes from the accuracy with which the policy construct will conceive of the object of its problematization. Meaning that a policy will be more effective at reducing certain types of drug-related harms, the better it conceptualizes the phenomenon it aims to deal with. In the specific case of addiction, and as I will develop later on, this means that a policy will be more effective if it operates under the conception of addiction as a brain disease, and not the conception of addicted persons as agents making irrational choices.

Harm reduction policy measures, as their name very aptly describes, aim not to eliminate a societal problem or the source of it, but rather to minimize the damage caused by the vices and problematic practices of certain people.

The concept of "harm reduction" as a policy strategy began to appear more frequently in academic literature towards the late 1980s and early 1990s, as a response to the epidemics of HIV infections going from injecting drug-users to the general population, that were affecting many countries at that time. As such, it is not a clearly defined set of policy protocols, but rather a general conceptual term.

The term "harm reduction" has never been defined by an official body. The bewildering variety of interpretations of this term adds to the confusion of an area already complicated by lack of terminological clarity and excessive emotional fervour. (Wodak, 1999, p. 169)

It is, historically speaking and in line with the aforementioned legislative narrative, a response to avowed failures of prohibitionist measures and can be seen as the moderate middle-ground between free-rein liberalism and harsh conservative criminalization stances. Be it in the realm of alcohol and tobacco, illegal drug use, or sex work, the strategies for harm reduction are motivated by the general premise that it will either be impossible or far too costly to implement measures that would completely eradicate the illegal drug trade or illicit sex industry and thus regulatory measures would better serve the public by focusing on reducing the levels of harm from these practices.

> Harm reduction can be described as a strategy directed toward individuals or groups that aims to reduce the harms associated with certain behaviours. When applied to substance abuse, harm reduction accepts that a continuing level of drug use (both licit and illicit) in society is inevitable and defines objectives as reducing adverse consequences. It emphasizes the measurement of health, social and economic outcomes, as opposed to the measurement of drug consumption.
>
> (Leslie, 2008, p. 53)

In encompassing licit substance abuse (i.e., alcohol and tobacco) as part of the strategies from harm reduction theory, there is also an acknowledgement of the notion that societal harm and criminality are not inextricably linked. Though harm reduction strategies can be applied to different behaviours, I will here focus only on the specific harm reduction policies aimed at minimizing the harm from illicit drug use.

Shifting the focus of policies towards reducing harm rather than eliminating criminal elements, there is a difference in the measure of a policy's effectiveness as well. Whereas the criminal focus can have fairly simple metrics for evaluating a policy's effect (e.g., number of arrests, quantity of illicit drugs seized, etc.), harm reduction policies have different subsets of goals that need to be defined in order to form the matrix of potential "effective" harm reduction outcomes. These goals can be organized through a hierarchy of decreasing the negative effects of drug use (Newcombe, 1992). As the term "harm reduction" appeared in the literature when describing the policy practices motivated by an attempt to limit the transmission of HIV infection among injection drug users (Advisory Council on Misuse of Drugs, 1988), the cascading goals in that area can range from the shift from injection to oral use, to a reduction in the number of times a user injects, to the cleaning of injection equipment before use, to the reduction of the number of people with whom the injection equipment is shared, and finally to the switch from an illicit drug being injected to medically prescribed alternatives (if not outright cessation of use). This is but one example of a hierarchy of goals in the subset of HIV transmission reduction goals. And as we can see, there are various points along that hierarchy where a reduction in any of those practices can be enough to consider the policy "effective", though the concept of harm and the actual metric by which it can be considered to have been *reduced* is an and of itself a murky area (Hunt & Stevens, 2004).

Though self-evident now, the political epistemological shift in this type of strategy is significant. In the harm reduction theory for illicit drug use, no longer are the products considered dangerous *unbeknownst* to the general populace, as is the case in the conception of drug use in the Pharmacy Act of 1868. Neither are substances in-and-of-themselves dangerous regardless of intent for moderate use, as is the notion behind the Dangerous Drugs Act of 1920. And finally, no longer are drug users, and particularly drug dealers, seen as the villains in the story, needing to be fought with harsh criminalization measures, as can still be considered the case in the Drugs Act of 2005 (Stevens, 2010). The shift towards harm reduction in the policy-construction discourse, over the past few decades, marks a change in the conception not only of the place of illicit drugs in society (a somewhat stoic acceptance that they are not going anywhere) but also of the very nature of the behaviour driving illicit drug use in the first place, of addiction itself. While a shift towards a more medically-focused perspective had already taken place in the late 19th century, harm reduction theory cements the notion that it is more effective, from a policy outcome standpoint, to consider the consumption of psychoactive substances as more akin to the behaviour of a patient than that of a criminal.

Furthermore, and as part of the argument that I propose in this book, a "harm reduction" theory is based upon an ethical consideration of the effects of the practices it aims to reduce. Indeed a harm reduction practice may be considered from a purely pragmatic perspective as a strategy for effectively reaching a stated goal (e.g., the reduction of transmission of HIV through needle distribution programs), but the motivation for its implementation is never value-neutral.

> ...advocates of harm reduction strategies argue not merely that they work, but that the fact that they work is a good thing. The implicit point is that

> harm (however identified) is something to be avoided or minimized and that—at least prima facie—a strategy that avoids or minimizes harm will be a good thing.
>
> (Kleinig, 2008, p. 4)

This of course does not absolve a harm reduction strategy from being critically assessed in its methods, and even though its stated goal may be desirable, the concrete practices put in place to achieve that goal must be ethically sound as well (Strang & Fortson, 2004). The consideration of the ethical implications of "harm reduction" practices goes even further. For while it may self-evident that a "reduction of harm" is an uncontroversially desirable outcome in any practice, what exactly constitutes a "harm" will inevitably be loaded with evaluative and normative considerations. Indeed, a detailed list of the reduced harms that might be accomplished may seem sufficient to justify a "harm reduction" strategy, but identifying and weighing harms can sometimes be a murkier endeavour ethically speaking. Consider the example of the Snowflakes Frozen Embryo Adoption Program (Belluck, 2005), which was initiated in the United States back in the early 2000s and consisted of the adoption of "leftover" embryos that were not used in *in vitro fertilization* (IVF) programs. While the people who launched this program would generally oppose IVF for moral or religious reasons concerning the sanctity of life, they believed that adopting an embryo was a lesser evil (i.e., a reduced harm) than having them be destroyed (or even worse in their estimation, used for stem cell research).

> It might be argued that whether or not a particular form of behavior has a determinate value is a function of the context in which it occurs and is not intrinsic to the activity itself. [...] Wherever behavior impacts on human interests, it is a candidate for evaluation, and it does not help the cause of harm reduction advocates to ignore this or to prescind from the debate about whether the impacted interests are deleteriously affected or on balance advanced.
>
> (Kleinig, 2008, p. 6)

Neither are "harm reduction" practices able to operate in a vacuum of ethical considerations. Rather, the motivation behind the implementation of a "harm reduction" practice may be that such a strategy will involve no value judgement of the underlying behaviour that is at the root of the harm being addressed.

> Such policies, it is claimed, make no judgment about adolescent sex or smoking or drug use or driving in certain ways. All that they do is affirm that the harms that are risked or caused by such practices, including any

> harms that might be involved in the practices themselves, will be reduced or minimized by such policies—whether they are condom distribution or needle and syringe exchange programs, seatbelt laws, or promotions of smokeless tobacco or nicotine patches.
>
> (Kleinig, 2008, p. 6)

Advocates of "harm reduction" policies will argue that a recognition of a societal behaviour does not imply its condonation, but rather that an acceptance of it as a reality will better serve the reduction of the harms it causes, and that such a reduction in harm outweighs the harm that may be perpetuated by the implementation of such practices.

> In other words there is a judgment about the relative weight that different harms are to be accorded, and that the manifest harms prevented by harm reduction policies make them preferable to whatever the status quo without such policies may be.
>
> (Kleinig, 2008, p. 6)

While there are many arguments for the implementation of harm reduction policies as viable alternatives to criminalization stances against illicit drug use, my aim in this chapter is not to provide any legal arguments for the decriminalization of illicit drug use, but rather to propose a distinction between two types of policy constructs and suggest that the varying levels of effectiveness that one may have over the other is linked to the philosophical adoption of the brain disease model paradigm in one (local harm reduction measures), while the rejection of it by the other (external criminalization edicts) has proven ineffective in reducing illicit drug use harm. Indeed, the theory behind "harm reduction" efforts is based largely on an ethical standpoint regarding harm reduction policies as more humane alternatives to punitive measures, and government reviews of UK drug policy date back as far as 2002 for an official enunciation of harm reduction as the shifting focus (UK Home Office, 2002).

Furthermore, while harm reduction theory has been firmly established within the policy literature for a few decades now, there is no single definition or policy-construction protocol for a "harm reducing policy". Rather, there is a general approach to harm reduction which prioritizes (as the name suggests) the reduction of harm over the prevention of drug use. Said harm can be considered at different levels (e.g., health, social, and economic) and can occur at equally different levels (e.g., individual, community, national, and international). Hence, the actual "harm" that a policy might reduce can range from an overdose death suffered by a drug user, a sense of safety from the illicit drug trade in a community, and economic costs to a society due to policing and medical expenses for illicit drug control.

When Reduction does More Harm

In 2018, the UK government set a significant public health goal, pledging that England would be "smokefree" by 2030. In practice, this ambitious target means reducing smoking rates to 5% or less by the year 2030. Scotland has also committed to a similar objective, albeit with a slightly extended timeline, aiming to achieve these lower smoking rates by 2034. These discussions and commitments have been influenced by comparable initiatives, such as the one proposed by New Zealand's government, which has set an even more aggressive goal of becoming a completely smoke-free country by 2025.

Both the United Kingdom and New Zealand's proposals draw inspiration from the World Health Organization's Tobacco Free Initiative. This global effort seeks to drastically reduce tobacco use and to provide the highest level of protection possible from the harmful effects of second-hand smoke. The overarching aim is to create a future where tobacco consumption is minimal and its associated risks are significantly reduced.

Reactions to these smokefree targets have been diverse, reflecting a range of perspectives across the political and social spectrum. While there is considerable support for these public health measures, there has also been notable resistance from some political analysts and commentators. It's important to highlight that the UK government's plan does not include the complete criminalization of tobacco product sales, instead focusing on reducing smoking prevalence through other means.

New Zealand's approach, on the other hand, is more stringent and includes a proposal that would ban the sale of tobacco products to individuals born after January 1, 2004. This "smokefree generation" policy would effectively prevent these new cohorts from ever legally purchasing smoked tobacco products, with the aim of phasing out tobacco use over time. If, for example, this legislation had been implemented on January 1, 2022, anyone younger than 18 at that time, or those born after January 1, 2004, would never be able to legally buy smoked tobacco products, marking a significant step towards a tobacco-free future.

Arguments against these proposals are varied, ranging from concerns about ageist discrimination to scepticism about the effectiveness of legal bans on psychoactive, addictive substances. Critics argue that such bans often lead to the creation of black markets rather than reducing consumption. For instance, South Africa's ban on alcohol sales during the COVID-19 crisis resulted in a sharp increase in people illegally producing their own alcohol, leading to significant health risks and unintended consequences.

There is also a historical dimension to these critiques, as such bans can be seen as historically myopic. The alcohol prohibition era in the United States during the 1920s is often cited as a classic example of the ineffectiveness of prohibitionist measures. The era not only failed to curb alcohol consumption but also led to the rise of organized crime syndicates, which capitalized on the illegal market, thereby exacerbating the social problems the ban sought to address.

Furthermore, these proposals seem to be at odds with recent and highly successful decriminalization approaches, such as Portugal's National Drug Strategy of 1999. Portugal's strategy focused on eliminating criminal penalties for personal drug possession, aiming instead to treat drug use as a public health issue rather than a criminal one. This approach has been praised globally for its success in reducing drug-related harm and its positive impact on society.

Some arguments against harsh punitive measures towards drugs highlight a perceived hypocrisy in focusing on illicit substances when alcohol and tobacco cause far greater harm to society. For instance, the Office for National Statistics in the United Kingdom reported that in 2019, there were 7,565 deaths related to alcohol-specific causes, the second highest since the data series began in 2001. This contrasts sharply with the 2,883 deaths related to drug misuse in the same year, a figure that includes dozens of illicit drugs controlled under the Misuse of Drugs Act 1971 combined. The disparity in the social and health costs of alcohol and tobacco compared to illicit drugs provides a strong argument against the harsh punitive measures often directed at the latter.

However, there is a potential danger in following this line of reasoning to its logical conclusion. A comparative argument between the harms of legal and illegal substances risks oversimplifying the complex issue of drug misuse and addiction. Individuals may turn to psychoactive substances for a variety of reasons, often to numb pain, suffering, or trauma, leading to self-medication. However, the decision-making process of someone addicted to drugs rarely involves weighing the relative risks of different substances. Many experts argue that legality alone is not a strong enough deterrent to prevent continued drug misuse among those struggling with addiction.

Given this context, it is understandable why some people are sceptical about the effectiveness of tobacco bans. Those who are addicted to nicotine or other substances are likely to continue seeking out these products, regardless of their legal status. Pushing them away from regulated, legal products towards underground, unregulated markets could expose them to even greater health and safety risks, potentially exacerbating the very issues these bans are intended to mitigate.

To be clear, the tobacco ban proposals, along with the WHO initiative from which they originate, are driven by good intentions. The primary goal is to prevent future generations from being exposed to harmful substances, thereby potentially improving their long-term health and reducing the burden of smoking-related diseases. By nipping the problem in the bud, these measures aim to create a healthier population in the years to come.

However, this raises significant questions about how such a ban would be enforced in practice. Even if these measures were effective in reducing tobacco use, concerns about authoritarianism and government overreach become prominent. Enforcement of strict bans often brings to mind the heavy-handed approaches seen in certain Southeast Asian countries, where drug laws are notoriously severe. In places like Singapore, for example, overreach by law enforcement and presumptions of intent to traffic drugs – offenses that can carry the death penalty – are frequently cited as abuses of power. Human rights organizations, such as Amnesty International, have long campaigned against these exaggerated sentencing practices, highlighting the dangers of strict enforcement measures.

Moreover, this debate raises another important question: What about other harmful but legal substances? The slippery slope argument becomes particularly relevant here. While it is clear that substances like alcohol and tobacco cause significant harm and contribute to thousands of deaths annually, other legal substances, such as refined sugar and high-calorie foods, are also major contributors to global health issues. Cardiovascular diseases (CVDs), for example, are the leading cause of death worldwide. In 2019 alone, an estimated 17.9 million people died from CVDs, accounting for 32% of all global deaths. These diseases are often linked to poor diets high in sugar and saturated fats.

Given these statistics, does banning tobacco on health grounds make a similar fate for refined sugar and high-fat foods more likely? It's not an unreasonable concern. In fact, the United Kingdom has already taken steps in this direction, albeit in a limited context. In 2006, a ban on fizzy drinks and junk food, including the now-infamous Turkey Twizzlers, was implemented in school canteens across the country. While this ban aimed to improve children's health, it did not extend to adults, nor was it a complete prohibition of these foods for all age groups.

Yet, even in this controlled environment, prohibition led to rule-breaking, with reports emerging of parents passing takeaway food to their children through school gates. This example highlights the challenges of enforcing bans, even on a small scale, and underscores the complexities of implementing broader restrictions on harmful substances.

Banning junk food for adults might seem like an overreach or even a nonsensical idea to many. However, it illustrates the underlying bioethical tensions in the debate surrounding tobacco bans. If individuals are considered old and mature enough to make decisions about their health, should they not have the right to choose, even if those choices are unhealthy or seemingly irrational? Do we, as a society, have the right to make unhealthy choices? These ethical concerns are central to the debate, yet they seem to be missing from many discussions about the proposed tobacco bans. It is this lack of consideration for individual autonomy and the right to make personal health decisions that makes the conversation around tobacco prohibition particularly contentious.

This is not an argument advocating for the complete absence of regulation, nor is it a defense of a libertarian state where the responsibility for collective public health is entirely delegated to individual choice. Public health requires thoughtful and balanced interventions to ensure the wellbeing of the population.

However, this is a call for considering alternative public health proposals that might be more effective in addressing the root causes of addiction. A stronger emphasis on the social determinants of health and the health outcomes associated with illness could yield more meaningful and sustainable results in combating addiction, all while avoiding the need to excessively restrict individual freedoms.

The WHO's Tobacco Free Initiative recognizes the importance of these social determinants – such as education, social and economic welfare, and broader measures of inequality – in shaping global health strategies. By focusing on these underlying factors, public health policies can be more targeted and equitable, addressing the real drivers of health disparities.

For instance, a report published in 2019 by the Norwegian Institute of Public Health highlighted stark differences in smoking rates across the Nordic countries (Iceland, Norway, Sweden, Finland, and Denmark). The data revealed that the percentage of smokers was up to four times higher among individuals with only primary education compared to those with degree-level education. This striking disparity underscores how educational attainment and socioeconomic status play crucial roles in health behaviours, including smoking.

Given this context, it is both troubling and worrisome that some governments are drafting policy goals that seek to create a "tobacco-free" society primarily through prohibitionist approaches. Such strategies risk overlooking the more fundamental public health measures that are essential for addressing the social and health inequalities that underpin tobacco addiction. By focusing on prohibition rather than reinforcing the public health infrastructure needed to tackle these inequalities, policymakers may inadvertently exacerbate the very problems they aim to solve.

A more nuanced and comprehensive approach, one that integrates efforts to improve education, reduce inequality, and enhance social welfare, could lead to more effective outcomes in the fight against tobacco addiction. Such an approach would not only respect individual freedoms but also address the broader social context in which addiction occurs, ultimately fostering a healthier and more equitable society.

Effectiveness of Harm Reduction Strategies

Throughout this chapter, I have tried to contextualize harm reduction strategies within the broader context of the evolution of UK drug policy. That history, as we've seen, is marked by shifts in societal attitudes towards substance abuse which are then translated into policy shifts, moving from punitive measures to more health-oriented approaches. This evolution demonstrates the recognition of addiction as a complex public health matter, rather than purely a criminal matter.

As I've recapitulated, the Misuse of Drugs Act of 1971 remains the cornerstone of UK drug policy, categorizing drugs into distinct classes based on their perceived harm and establishing the legal framework for drug control. However, over the decades, the rigid punitive stance has faced criticism for failing to address the underlying issues of addiction and its social determinants. This criticism has given rise to harm reduction strategies, which aim to minimize the negative consequences of drug use without necessarily reducing drug consumption, firstly as a policy construct emerging during the 1980s as a response to the HIV/AIDS epidemic. As I've already mentioned, needle exchange programs were introduced to reduce the transmission of blood-borne viruses among injecting drug users. This approach marked a departure from the abstinence-focused policies of the past, acknowledging that some individuals would continue to use drugs and that minimizing harm was a more attainable goal.

To really measure the effectiveness of harm reduction strategies, it's important to compare different approaches both within the United Kingdom and internationally. The United Kingdom's experience can be juxtaposed with places like Portugal, Switzerland, Canada, and San Francisco, which have implemented harm reduction policies within different socio-political contexts.

In the United Kingdom, harm reduction strategies have been somewhat successful in reducing drug-related harms. For instance, the widespread availability of needle exchange programs has been instrumental in curbing the spread of HIV among injecting drug users. The introduction of opioid substitute therapies, particularly methadone and buprenorphine, has helped stabilize the lives of individuals with opioid dependence, reducing their involvement in criminal activities and improving their health outcomes.

However, the United Kingdom's harm reduction efforts have faced some challenges. The recent austerity measures implemented in the 2010s led to significant cuts in public health funding, adversely affecting harm reduction services. The closure of several needle exchange program sites and a lack of investment in new interventions, such as supervised drug consumption rooms, have impacted the effectiveness of harm reduction strategies.

In contrast, Portugal's policy of decriminalization of all drugs in 2001 is often cited as a successful harm reduction model. By shifting the focus from criminalization to public health, Portugal saw a dramatic reduction in drug-related deaths, HIV infection rates, and overall drug use. The country's approach included comprehensive harm reduction services, such as needle exchange programs, opioid substitution therapies, and social reintegration programs, which were part of a broader strategy to address the environmental determinants of drug abuse.

The success of Portugal's model lies in its holistic approach, which could be labelled as a sort of "proto-biopsychosocial model", combining harm reduction with prevention, treatment, and social support. The decriminalization policy has not only reduced the burden on the criminal justice system but also destigmatized drug users, encouraging more individuals to seek help.

Switzerland's harm reduction strategy is yet another example of a comprehensive approach to addiction and drug-related issues. The country's supervised drug consumption rooms, introduced in the 1980s, have been effective in reducing drug-related deaths and improving the health of people who consume psychoactive substances. Switzerland also implemented heroin-assisted treatment for individuals with severe opioid dependence, which has proven successful in reducing illicit drug use, criminal behaviour, and health complications associated with drug use (Uchtenhagen, 2010).

Switzerland's model is characterized by its emphasis on public health and human rights, ensuring that drug users have access to safe, dignified, and effective care. The country's success highlights the importance of integrating harm reduction into a broader public health strategy, supported by adequate resources and political will.

On the other end of the effectiveness spectrum, Canada's approach to harm reduction, particularly in cities like Vancouver, has garnered global attention for its progressive policies, such as the establishment of INSITE, North America's first legally sanctioned supervised injection site, which opened in 2003. These measures had been effective in reducing overdose deaths, the spread of infectious diseases, and public drug use. However, the country has recently faced criticism for its unintended negative outcomes.

One of the major issues in Canada has been the surge in opioid-related deaths despite the availability of harm reduction services. The introduction of potent synthetic opioids like fentanyl into the drug supply has exacerbated the crisis, leading to a dramatic increase in overdoses. Critics have argued that while harm reduction services are crucial, they are insufficient in addressing the root causes of addiction, such as mental health issues, poverty, and social isolation (Smye et al., 2011).

San Francisco is unfortunately another city that has embraced harm reduction, a measure that was long-due in response to its issues with drug addiction and homelessness, but which has not had overwhelmingly positive results in the long run. The city has implemented a range of harm reduction services, including needle exchange programs, supervised drug consumption rooms, and the distribution of naloxone, an opioid overdose reversal drug. But despite these efforts, San Francisco has struggled with the unintended consequences of its policies. The city has seen a rise in open drug use, with critics arguing that harm reduction has inadvertently enabled public drug consumption and contributed to the visibility of the drug crisis. Additionally, the focus on harm reduction has been criticized for diverting attention and resources away from long-term solutions, such as comprehensive treatment and rehabilitation programs. The city's homelessness crisis, which is often intertwined with substance use disorders, has further complicated the effectiveness of harm reduction efforts, leading to growing public frustration and demands for a more balanced approach.

As we can see, the efficacy of harm reduction strategies should be evaluated on several criteria, including health outcomes, social integration, and cost-effectiveness. While in the United Kingdom, harm reduction interventions have demonstrated positive health outcomes, such as reductions in HIV transmission and drug-related deaths, the full potential of harm reduction has been undermined internationally by inconsistent policy implementation, inadequate funding, and political resistance to more progressive measures.

Comparing the United Kingdom's approach with those of Portugal, Switzerland, Canada, and San Francisco reveals the importance of a cohesive and well-funded harm reduction strategy. The successes and challenges in these places highlight the need for the United Kingdom to adopt a more integrated approach, combining harm reduction with prevention, treatment, and social support services.

The United Kingdom should invest in the expansion of harm reduction services, including the establishment of supervised drug consumption rooms and the provision of drug checking services. But these practices should be integrated into a broader public health strategy that addresses the social determinants of drug use. They require collaboration between healthcare providers, social services, and community organizations; and in order to achieve the desired outcomes, these harm reduction services must be adequately funded. It goes without saying that a reversal of the austerity cuts and a prioritization of investment in public health, recognizing the long-term benefits of harm reduction for individuals and society, would be the first step in this direction.

This idea goes hand in hand with the fact that policymaking should be guided by evidence rather than ideology. The United Kingdom can learn from the successes of countries like Portugal and Switzerland, while also acknowledging the challenges faced by Canada and San Francisco, adapting their approaches to the local context while maintaining a commitment to evidence-based practices.

As I hope to demonstrate in the following section, the effectiveness of harm reduction strategies in addressing drug-related issues in the United Kingdom is contingent upon their integration into a comprehensive public health policy framework. And one important step in this direction is the recognition of the distinction between different policy constructs, and the overriding ideology behind each.

Distinguishing Between Constructs

As I mentioned in the overview of what "harm reduction" practices consider an "effective" outcome, there is a cascading list of harms that can be reduced.

If we were to consider a pure cost-effectiveness view of "harm reduction", we could see that less public resources spent on prosecution and incarceration for minor drug offences would be reduced harm to the public good. Yet, that is not the only harm, nor is it the most important harm from which to build an ethical argument. A consideration of the fact that incarceration for a minor drug offence is inherently wrong need be the only factor to consider in evaluating whether a practice has sufficiently reduced harm, if it lowers the rate of incarceration for minor drug offences (ignoring the addendum of less public resources being wasted). With that in mind, the example I will use later on will focus on a reduction in the number of overdose deaths from opioid substances, considering that regardless of the illicit nature of the substance and the stigma that may surround the social practice of consuming opioid and opioid derivatives, it is a good thing that less people die from the practice, and that any policy put in place that allows for "harm reduction" practices to reduce that number of deaths is by that very fact a better alternative, ethically speaking, than a punitive measure which doesn't help reduce that number of deaths.

Considering this kaleidoscopic view of the different harms that a policy construct may try to reduce, it is easy to see how one might feel at a loss in terms of guidance regarding the way in which policy constructs should arbitrate between programs that might influence harm at different levels and for different subsets of people within the population, namely drug users and non-drug users (Tsui, 2000). Indeed, there may be little overlap in the types of programs and spending allocations for policy measures that would aim to reduce harm in the areas of individual health, public safety, and reduction of public resource spending. Consequently, in my distinction between policy constructs and my argument regarding higher effectiveness in harm reduction for one over the other, I will focus on harm reduction for addicted persons and will measure the effectiveness of policy construct with regard to how efficient they are in reducing harm for the individual and collective subsets of illicit drug users. As I have mentioned before, this goes hand in hand with the ethical claim of this book, which is that a more effective method of reducing harm is in-and-of-itself a good thing, and ought to be promoted not only on the grounds that it is more effective, but also that it is a more ethical foundation for the treatment of addicted persons by policy.

The distinction I will make between policy constructs is not an official distinction, nor is it an established taxonomic method of differentiating one type of policy from another. Rather, my argument stems from the interdisciplinary link between the neuroscientific paradigm of addiction as a brain disease and the type of public health policy which adopts this paradigm into its underlying rationale for the implementation of harm reduction strategies. In the broadest sense, my distinction is between policy constructs and their point of origin. The point of making distinction is grounded in the argument that one policy construct will be more effective in reducing drug-related harms, which I also argue is the more ethical option in terms of the treatment of addicted persons. On the one hand, we have policies whose point of origin is at the local community level (sometimes being as specific as one singular clinical trial) and whose moderate success gives way to further and broader adoption of its protocol, finally reaching the level of national policy and achieving supranational status by being studied in comparative international policy reviews, thus becoming a model followed by other countries. I call this type of construct "Local to External" (L-E). The second type of policy is simply the reverse, by which I mean an international edict, which will generally come from an intergovernmental organization like the United Nations or any of its specialized agencies, like the World Health Organization, and which will be adopted at the national level (Federal or State) by each country, then to be diluted down to local enforcement protocols in communities. I call this type of construct "External to Local" (E-L).[2]

External Policy Constructs

In order to better flesh out my argument, I will discuss one notable example from each of these two types of constructs and provide arguments for the effectiveness in reducing harm to addicted persons for each. Beginning with E-L constructs, let's take one of the most notable examples: cannabis. Until December 2020, the official stance on the international regulation of cannabis by the UN Commission on Narcotic Drugs (CND) was to classify it as a Schedule IV type of substance, according to the 1961 Single Convention on Narcotic Drugs. This is to say that less than a month ago (at the time of writing this chapter), the international verdict on cannabis was that it was as dangerous as heroin. After a somewhat narrow vote (27 in favour, 25 against, out of the CND's 53 Member States), the medicinal and therapeutic properties of the plant were recognized to outweigh its potential health risk (in what could be argued was a consideration of the relative harms caused by prohibition vs. legality, though not entirely in the theoretical framework of "harm reduction" per se). Furthermore, Canada, Uruguay, and Mexico have now extended the legality of cannabis for recreational use as well.

This development comes after more than half a century of local drug policy in all 53 Member States taking its cue from the 1961 Single Convention wherein cannabis was declared to be a considerable risk to public health, and its production and distribution were strictly prohibited. It is beyond the scope of this chapter to provide a detailed history of the tumultuous struggle that cannabis users have waged against staunch prohibitionist stances for all these years. Suffice it to say, there is a vast array of works that delve into the sociopolitical ramifications of the 1961 Single Convention (Monaghan, 2014), as well as the different influences and impact that the political discourse, particularly during the Civil Rights movement of the 1960s in the United States, had on the policy constructs used to regulate and control cannabis, the impacts of which have been evidently long-lasting (Hudak, 2020).

In tracing the history of the policies put in place to regulate cannabis, my aim is not to exhaust the analytical avenues for the study of the political ramifications of prohibiting the use of cannabis *per se*, but rather to show how ineffective policies, and by all accounts they have been ineffective (Stevens 2010), can be traced back to international influence. In the case of UK drug policy, the Misuse of Drugs Act of 1971 came about as a direct consequence of international pressure for the United Kingdom to put into action various treaty commitments made at the 1961 Single Convention on Narcotic Drugs, thus reflecting in concrete policy terms the classification of cannabis as a Schedule IV dangerous substance. Before 1971, the UK had a relatively more liberal drugs policy, at least with regard to cannabis, and it wasn't until the United Nations' pressure that cannabis became such a harsh criminalized drug offence in the United Kingdom.

Needless to say, such a classification has been demonstrated to be the product of historical assumptions (Hudak, 2020) and ignores the scientific evidence for its medicinal and therapeutic benefits, even by appointed government committees dedicated to the question (UK House of Commons, 2006). Once again, the aim of this chapter is not to provide any further arguments against the criminalization of cannabis but rather to suggest that the policy constructs put in place to regulate it were ineffective in reducing whatever harm was thought to be caused by it.

In their 2010 book, "Cannabis Policy: Moving Beyond Stalemate", Room et al. review the impacts that the international prohibitionist measures against cannabis have had on society. They summarize the unsuccessful attempts at limiting use thusly:

> Despite its prohibition in every country apart from the Netherlands, experimentation with cannabis is a routine experience among adolescents in many Western nations. Use is more common among males than females, but even among females a large proportion has tried the drug by their early adult years. A substantial fraction of those who experiment go on to use the drug frequently, and a modest share of those experience problems of dependence. The rates of experimentation vary considerably across countries at the same level of economic development, probably reflecting broad cultural and social factors.
>
> (Room et al., 2010, p. 53)

Assessing whether the criminalization policies in most Western countries have had the results that were explicitly sought in the UN conventions from which the international prohibitionist regime took its cues, it is argued by Room et al. that almost no significant impact has been achieved:

> Regarding impacts of reforms on prevalence of cannabis use, it is also apparent from a number of the studies that, at least as long as the illegality of cannabis is maintained, the laws and sanctions which apply seem to have, at most, a relatively modest impact on rates of cannabis use. In a number of examples, trends in cannabis use appear to be independent of the penalties which apply. It is likely that, as far as reforms under the existing international treaties are concerned, other non-legal factors such as social, economic, and cultural trends, some of which exert their influence across state and national boundaries, have a far greater impact on cannabis use than the penalties which apply in a particular jurisdiction to that very small proportion of users who are ever arrested.
>
> (Room et al., 2010, p. 127)

The argument that must be gleaned from this example is that the policies that came from an external source, the UN conventions and the "War on Drugs" ideology of the late 20th century, were trickled down to local policies that ignored the science and evidence for the consideration of cannabis use as something other than a criminal behaviour, which produced social and political inequalities (Stevens, 2010), led to mass incarceration of young males in the United States, and stigmatized a practice which dates back millennia, has demonstrable medicinal properties and by some estimates is consumed by 4% of the adult population of the world, as reported by the figures from the UN Office on Drugs and Crime (UNODC), which indicated that in 2006–2007 some 166 million people aged 15 or above used cannabis.

Local Policy Constructs

Take-Home Naloxone Kits and the Reduction of Overdose Deaths in Scotland

In sharp contrast with this, I now turn to what I understand by L-E policy constructs. To do so, I will use the example of the Take-Home Naloxone overdose prevention kits in Scotland, a national policy that began life as an op-ed article suggesting the idea of naloxone as a potential peer administration intervention possibility, back in 1992 (Strang & Farrell, 1992). This idea evolved, took the form of various other peer-reviewed studies (Strang et al., 1996; Strang et al., 1999), and was reviewed by the Scottish Advisory Committee on Drug Misuse (SACDM, 2005), followed by legal amendments to the Medicines Act in 2005 that paved the way for a pilot study to be conducted in three local areas in 2007 (Armstrong, Jarvie, Scott, & Robson, 2007). Following the success of these programs, the National Program in

Scotland was officially launched in 2010, with the Scottish Government approving public funding to Health Boards for 6,000 kits in 2012 (Scottish Government, 2011). The success of the program led to its implementation in other countries around the world, to the point that the CDC estimates that, as of 2014, 26,000 cases of opioid overdoses had been reversed as a direct consequence of the THN kits (Wheeler et al., 2015). Naloxone is on the World Health Organization's List of Essential Medicines (WHO, 2017), which counts the most effective and safe medicines needed in a health system.

Implicit in the design and impetus behind this program (and explicit in the articles describing the reasoning behind it) is the conception of addiction as a brain disease, and thus a problem to be solved in the realm of medicine and public health rather than that of the criminal justice system. The view that addiction is a neurobiologically observable disease may be critically assessed, given that it establishes a deterministic worldview, may fail to account for heterogeneity in remission rates, may place too much emphasis on the compulsive aspect of addictive behaviour, and may lack a specific neural signature that would provide a clear method of diagnosis. Yet, the foundational premise that addiction has a neurobiological basis is what motivates "harm reduction" efforts such as the THN program, in that it considers addiction as a disorder requiring access to healthcare and treatment. Specifically, and in line with the theory behind "harm reduction", the premise of this program is that a prevalent addiction to opioids in society may be an undesirable phenomenon and that it is a situation which ought to change. However, while such a prevalent situation exists, and if one harmful consequence of an opioid addiction is the risk of an overdose death, then any practice that could actively reduce that risk is a good thing and should be promoted. The motivation behind this particular program, and the design of the pilot studies from which the program originated, took into account local behavioural patterns, adopted a clinical perspective on the oversight and follow-up protocols for the observation of the impact of the THN kits, rather than a judicial one, and thus was able to provide encouraging data for its implementation to be broadened nationally. The concept of "effectiveness" may need further unpacking with regard to the reduction in levels of harm from addiction, but it is evident that this particular measure has been effective in actively reducing a particular harm caused by addiction (i.e., overdose death).

PMA and the Link between UK Drug Policy and Overdose Deaths

In early 2015, a sharp rise in overdose deaths occurring from the drug paramethoxyamphetamine (PMA), brought about a conversation concerning the risk of methamphetamine derivatives, since it was believed the allure of this drug was its similar effects to 3,4-methylenedioxy-methamphetamine, more commonly known as MDMA. The pills in question were nicknamed "Superman Pills" due to their design logo and were believed to be consumed in full knowledge of their chemical composition. This was not the case, rather the overdose deaths seemed to come from the inadvertent consumption of PMA by persons believing they had purchased ecstasy pills (MDMA).

As explained by Professor David Nutt:

> PMA/PMMA are significantly more toxic than MDMA for three reasons. First they are more potent, up to 10 times so. This means that a user who is typically safely using MDMA at a dose of 80mg per session will be taking the equivalent of 800mg of MDMA if they take 80mg of PMA. Secondly, PMA works more slowly than MDMA so when users don't get the expected effects of MDMA about 30 minutes after taking the drug they think they have been sold a weak lot and may take another dose to make up for this. Then, when the effects of PMA kick in at around two hours, they have taken far too much. Thirdly PMA and PMMA are not pharmacological equivalents of MDMA. They have very different actions, which is why they were discarded after first testing. Their major problem is that they block the actions of the brain enzymes that offset the desired effects of serotonin and dopamine release that PMA/PMMA produce. This then massively accentuates their toxicity as the brain can't compensate for the increase in serotonin so users can develop serotonin syndrome. This is a toxic reaction that elevates body temperature to a dangerous, and in some cases lethal, level.
>
> (Nutt, 2015)

These reasons, higher potency, slower reaction time, and different pharmacological action in the brain made PMA a much more dangerous drug than MDMA. The real reason for this sudden uptick in overdose deaths by PMA, however, was in fact drug policy that banned certain chemicals from being used in the production chain for MDMA. These bans were a direct result of the UN drug control conventions and as such created a direct catalyst for the use of different precursor chemicals in the production of ecstasy, which resulted in PMA.

As Nutt further explains:

> Their re-emergence is directly due to the international community's attempts, via UN conventions, to stop the use of MDMA by prohibiting its production and sale. As the earlier UN drug control conventions were clearly not working, in 1988 a further attempt to limit drug use by impairing production was made by banning a number of precursor chemicals. One of these is safrole, the precursor of MDMA. In 2010 there was a massive seizure of 50 tonnes of safrole in Thailand. This did significantly

> dent availability for MDMA production, so chemists looked for an alternative source of a suitable precursor. Aniseed oil seemed the ideal alternative, as it is chemically very similar to safrole, so this was used. Unfortunately the product that results from using the MDMA production process with aniseed oil is PMA or PMMA. Hence these substances only exist because of the blockade of MDMA production. That in itself wouldn't particularly matter if they were not more toxic than MDMA.
>
> (Nutt, 2015)

This inadvertent result of the introduction of a far more potent chemical drug (PMA) than the target of the UN convention bans (MDMA) puts into sharp focus one of the realities of the war on drugs: prohibition and legal enforcement of bans will always be playing catch-up to the black markets of psychoactive substances. And the efforts and resources directed towards seizing illegal drugs and banning the elements used in the production of synthetic drugs will only create new markets or new means of production, sometimes with fatal consequences as was the case of the inadvertent result in PMA from the attempted ban on chemical elements used to create MDMA.

Furthermore, this case of inadvertent PMA resulting in overdose deaths not only showcases the fact that severe criminal penalties and prohibitionist stances on drug policy have adverse effects, but also equally demonstrates that more public health-oriented policies can be more effective in minimizing the harmful effects of such synthetic drugs like PMA. The Trimbos Institute, created in 1996 from a merger of the Netherlands Center for Mental Health (NCGv) and the Netherlands Institute for Alcohol and Drugs (NIAD), is dedicated to informing policymakers and professionals about issues regarding mental health and its comorbidities with drug abuse and addiction among the population in the Netherlands. It monitors and signals psychological and addiction problems and provides courses and training in the field of mental health care and addiction care, to support care providers in improving the quality of their work. Regarding the "Superman Pills" and the PMA overdose deaths in 2015, the Trimbos Institute had issued an alert regarding the dangers of these synthetic drugs containing different chemicals and being mistaken for ecstasy pills (DutchNews, 2014). Many scientists and drug policy advocates manifested the need for a closer look in the United Kingdom. The UK government evidently failed to act on that information.

It is impossible to say whether harm reduction strategies, such as those implemented by the Trimbos Institute, would have prevented all overdose deaths from PMA from happening, but it is safe to assume that statistically significantly fewer deaths would have occurred from the mistaking of PMA for ecstasy pills, if centres such as the drug testing centre in the Netherlands would have been available to the UK population, as some studies have shown a significant change in consumers' intention to use a substance which has been tested by drug testing facilities and shown to have contained a different chemical composition than the one consumers thought they had (Saleemi et al., 2017).

> *This finding that MDMA-negative pill-testing results led to lower rates of intention to use, suggests that pill testing may be effective in reducing consumption of unknown substances and decreasing related harms.*
>
> (Saleemi et al., 2017, p. 1059)

Drug testing facilities, where the public may have their illicit substances tested without fear of criminal prosecution, is an initiative that has slowly become adopted in other countries and has been slowly gaining traction in the United Kingdom (WEDINOS, 2021), though far slower than would be ideal.

The inherent distinction between a government reform on long-standing drug policy and localized practices such as drug-testing sites and safe-injection centres is the top-down/bottom-up approach to solving the immediate crisis of overdose deaths and harmful consequences of substance abuse. In this specific case of drug-testing facilities and the UN ban on the pre-cursor chemical for MDMA, we have an example of an L-E approach towards the reduction of a particular harm of addiction, and a particular case study which showcases the effectiveness of strategies such as drug-testing in alerting the public of potentially harmful drugs in the market, and thus avoiding unnecessary deaths due to the consumption of dangerous substances, while in the very same case, the Government's prohibitionist approach to the seizure of the chemical precursor is a clear example of a directive taken straight from UN conventions, an example of an E-L strategy, which only paved the way for the inadvertent creation of a more harmful substance and an increased risk of negative consequences, perhaps even the indirect result of the overdose deaths due to unknown PMA consumption.

Conclusion

The objective of this final chapter has been to show that there are differences between policy constructs that conceptualize addiction as a disorder with a neurobiological basis and policy constructs which adopt a "moral choice" model of addiction. Concretely speaking, these differences can be seen in the success that local "harm reduction" practices have had in reducing mortality rates, promoting better health outcomes for persons suffering from addiction, and ultimately destigmatizing dependence on psychoactive substances. Whereas punitive measures that have followed a policy construct set out by international edicts have been largely unsuccessful in their avowed goals of reducing consumption, disincentivizing distribution, and eradicating the world of drugs.

The examples I have mentioned in this book are by no means exhaustive, nor do they pretend to encompass the full picture of UK drug policy constructs and the different dynamics at play in influencing and determining their origin. I've chosen to focus on "harm reduction" strategies for I believe they fit into the narrative of legislative events that have shaped the evolution of the different conceptions of the problem of addiction in liberal governance, but it is important to note that many other types of policy constructs exist and continue to be debated and deliberated in public and private forums among policymakers.

My objective has been to provide an argument of a different kind for these types of policy strategies, namely that their effectiveness is rooted in the fact that they start locally and thus that they are more capable of incorporating a comprehensive and understanding approach to the problems of addiction in communities. In doing so, I argue that they adopt a paradigm of addiction as a brain disease that more aptly conveys the realities that local communities suffering from addiction are going through, which is why these policies are better poised to be more effective in reducing the harms of addiction.

Note

1 Source: UK Government Drugs penalties and sentencing, https://www.gov.uk/penalties-drug-possession-dealing.

References

Armstrong, E.M., Jarvie, A., Scott, W., & Robson, G. (2007). Patient Group Directions. Retrieved from http://www.sehd.scot.nhs.uk/mels/HDL2001_07.HTM

Belluck, P. (2005). From Stem Cell Opponents An Embryo Crusade. *New York Times*, 2 June 2005.

Berridge, V. (1978a). Professionalization and Narcotics: The Medical and Pharmaceutical Professions and British Narcotic Use 1868–1926. *Psychological Medicine*, *8*(3), 361–372.

Berridge, V. (1978b). War Conditions and Narcotics Control: The Passing of Defence of the Realm Act Regulation 40B. *Journal of Social Policy*, *7*(3), 285–304.

Berridge, V. (1999). Histories of Harm Reduction: Illicit Drugs, Tobacco, and Nicotine. *Substance Use & Misuse*, *34*(1), 35–47.

Drug Enforcement Administration. (2009). Methamphetamine http://www.usdoj.gov/dea/concern/meth.html.

Hudak, J. (2020). *Marijuana: A Short History*. Brookings Institution Press.

Hunt, N., & Stevens, A. (2004). Whose Harm? Harm Reduction and the Shift to Coercion in UK Drug Policy. *Social Policy and Society*, *3*(4), 333.

Kleinig, J. (2008). The Ethics of Harm Reduction. *Substance Use & Misuse*, *43*(1), 1–16. https://doi.org/10.1080/10826080701690680

Leslie, K. (2008). Harm Reduction: An Approach to Reducing Risky Health Behaviours in Adolescents. *Paediatrics & Child Health*, *13*(1), 53. https://doi.org/10.1093/pch/13.1.53

Marlatt, G.A., Larimer, M.E., & Witkiewitz, K. (Eds.). (2011). *Harm Reduction: Pragmatic Strategies for Managing High-Risk Behaviors*. Guilford Press.

Monaghan, M. (2014). Drug Policy Governance in the UK: Lessons from Changes to and Debates Concerning the Classification of Cannabis under the 1971 Misuse of Drugs Act. *International Journal of Drug Policy*, *25*(5), 1025–1030.

Newcombe, R. (1992). The Reduction of Drug-Related Harm: A Conceptual Framework for Theory, Practice and Research. In P. O'Hare, R. Newcombe, A. Matthews, and E.C. Buning (Eds.), *The Reduction of Drug Related Harm*, London: Routledge.

Nutt, D. (2015, June 5). The dangers of PMA and PMMA in ecstasy and 'legal highs'. The Conversation. Retrieved from https://theconversation.com/the-dangers-of-pma-and-pmma-in-ecstasy-and-legal-highs-42615

Room, R., Fischer, B., Hall, W., Lenton, S., Reuter, P., & Feilding, C.A. (2010). *Cannabis Policy: Moving Beyond Stalemate*. Oxford University Press, Incorporated.

Saleemi, S., Pennybaker, S.J., Wooldridge, M., & Johnson, M.W. (2017). Who is 'Molly'? MDMA Adulterants by Product Name and the Impact of Harm-Reduction Services at Raves. *Journal of Psychopharmacology*, *31*(8), 1056–1060. https://doi.org/10.1177/0269881117715596

Scottish Advisory Committee on Drug Misuse (SACDM). (2005). *Working Group On Drug Related Deaths: Report and Recommendations*. Edinburgh: Scottish Executive.

Scottish Government. (2011). Lord Advocate's Guidelines on Allowing the Supply of Naloxone to Extend to Staff Working for Services in Contact with People at Risk of Opiate Overdoses. Retrieved from http://www.sdf.org.uk/sdf/files/LordAdvocatesGuidelines.pdf

Skewes, M.C., & Gonzalez, V.M. (2013). The Biopsychosocial Model of Addiction. *Principles of Addiction*, *1*, 61–70.

Smye, V., Browne, A.J., Varcoe, C., & Josewski, V. (2011). Harm Reduction, Methadone Maintenance Treatment and the Root Causes of Health and Social Inequities: An Intersectional Lens in The Canadian Context. *Harm Reduction Journal*, *8*, 1–12.

Stevens, A. (2010). *Drugs, Crime and Public Health: The Political Economy of Drug Policy*. Routledge.

Strang, J., & Farrell, M. (1992). Harm Minimisation for Drug Misusers. *BMJ: British Medical Journal*, *304*(6835), 1127.

Strang, J., & Fortson, R. (2004). Supervised Fixing Rooms, Supervised Injectable Maintenance Clinics--Understanding The Difference. *BMJ (Clinical research ed.)*, *328*(7431), 102–103. https://doi.org/10.1136/bmj.328.7431.102

Strang, J., Darke, S., Hall, W., Farrell, M., & Ali, R. (1996). Heroin Overdose: The Case For Take-Home Naloxone.

Strang, J., Powis, B., Best, D., Vingoe, L., Griffiths, P., Taylor, C., et al. (1999). Preventing Opiate Overdose Fatalities With Take-Home Naloxone: Pre-Launch Study Of Possible Impact And Acceptability. *Addiction*, *94*(2), 199–204.

Tsui, M.S. (2000). The Harm Reduction Approach Revisited – An International Perspective. *International Social Work*, *43*(2), 243–251.

Uchtenhagen, A. (2010). Heroin-Assisted Treatment In Switzerland: A Case Study In Policy Change. *Addiction*, *105*(1), 29–37.

UK Home Office. (2002). *Updated Drug Strategy 2002*. Home Office.

UK House of Commons. (2006). Science and Technology Committee, 5th Report Session.

WEDINOS. (2021). Philtre Annual Report: 2020–21.

Wheeler, E., Jones, T.S., Gilbert, M.K., & Davidson, P.J. (2015). Opioid Overdose Prevention Programs Providing Naloxone To Laypersons—United States, 2014. *MMWR. Morbidity And Mortality Weekly Report*, *64*(23), 631.

WHO. (2017). *Model List of Essential Medicines, 20th list.* Geneva: World Health Organization. Available from: http://www.who.int/medicines/publications/essential medicines/20th_EML2017.pdf?ua=1

Wodak, A. (1999). What is this Thing Called Harm Reduction. *International Journal of Drug Policy*, *10*(3), 169–171.

DutchNews.nl. (2014, December 11) Drugs monitor issues warning for dangerous 'Superman' ecstasy pills. Retrieved from https://www.dutchnews.nl/2014/12/drugs-monitor-issues-warning-for-dangerous-superman-ecstasy-pills/

Conclusion

On Conceptualizing Addiction

The conceptualization of addiction has been a highly controversial subject in recent years. When it was first introduced, the brain disease model of addiction (BDMA) was seen as a sharp contrast to the prevailing moralistic and stigmatizing view of addiction as a condition resulting from poor decision-making. These stigmatizing views created barriers for addicted persons to access medical treatment and the proper tools for recovery. Neuroscientists had to argue that there was a neurobiological basis underlying their condition in order for them to be seen as "suffering from" addiction, instead of "choosing to" engage in their addiction. This argument was targeted at evidence-based policymakers and healthcare professionals, many of whom held strong beliefs regarding addiction as a disorder of choice.

The binary debate over addiction as either a neurobiological disease or a disorder of irrational choice-making should be re-understood as a discussion between two sides of the same coin. Both perspectives can inform their conceptualization of addiction and can be complementary to each other. In other words, it is possible to conceive of addiction as a brain disease which affects a person's faculties and ability to make choices. More specifically, we can understand addiction as a disorder that affects the central nervous system leading to dysregulated choice preferences that overvalue immediate reward reinforcement, a condition that is prone to peaks and valleys of relapse, and within which pre-existing genetic vulnerabilities and continuous psychoactive substance consumption can lead to a pronounced disruption in the brain circuitry that impairs and undermines agential capacities for adaptive behaviour but crucially does not nullify them completely.

What I have attempted to do in this book is argue that this conceptualization matters not only in destigmatizing the condition of addicted persons but also for policy constructs that operate under the model of addiction as a brain disease, because this conceptualization leads to a more effective type of harm reduction policies and as such is a more ethical treatment of addicted persons. The premise of my argument is that any useful conceptualization of

DOI: 10.4324/9781003582908-7

addiction requires a multidimensional approach and specifically an understanding of the brain neurocircuitry involved and how the environmental factors of an individual will interact with that brain. Crucially, however, I have taken care to avoid the trap of neuroreductionism, and I have attempted to place a neuroscientific perspective as a distinct part of the entire biopsychosocial understanding of addiction, which incorporates psychological, social, and economic processes into the holistic understanding of the addiction phenomenon.

In order to accentuate the importance of the conceptualization of addiction, I began this book with a concern over the philosophical conception of addictive behaviour, discussing the nature of action itself and why it was an important foundation for the specific case study of addictive action. This was followed by the contrasting view of addiction as a neurobiologically observable disruption of the neurocircuitry involved in reward, self-control, and compulsion. Addressing the problematic nature of viewing addiction as a brain disease in a fully deterministic fashion, I attempted to mitigate this neuroreductionism with a discussion on the philosophy of science and what neuroscience can and cannot tell us regarding human action.

The role of neuroscientific research into addiction need not be to diagnose more precisely the exact condition of addiction, but rather to improve our knowledge and understanding of this particular disorder and the mechanisms that underlie it. Hopefully, these mechanistic insights will provide pathways for new methods of treatment and personalized approaches to specific medical strategies to offset the physiological symptoms of withdrawal. Indeed a neuroscientific understanding of addiction was a necessary step in my argumentative structure, for it allowed me to situate it within a broader scope of the political environment within which addiction is dealt with in society. Public health policies, substance production and availability, as well as other socioeconomic factors, are critically important determinants of addiction. In this landscape, the brain can be a focal point of research and treatment but will serve a much greater goal if it drives coherent policy constructs aimed at dealing with addicted persons.

On Avoiding Easy Answers from Neuroreductionism

There is an undeniable appeal in a neuroreductionist worldview. This field of scientific research has made great advances and given us the ability to materially observe the physical and chemical processes that underlie addictive behaviour in the brain. Neuroimaging techniques allow us to see brain circuits actually light up when someone consumes a psychoactive substance of experiences a similar addictive craving. These techniques have provided invaluable information and thus inevitably have pushed the BDMA to the forefront of the conversation around this phenomenon. By focusing on elements like changes in dopamine signalling or alterations in the structure of the prefrontal cortex, researchers have built a strong case for the argument that addiction is far from being solely a question of moral failure or lack of self-control. It can be thought of as a disease with a very much observable biological foundation.

However, this very clarity is a double-edged sword. The neuroreductionist approach, by focusing so much on the dysfunctions observed in the brain, risks an oversimplification of a much more complex and layered disorder. Yes, addiction can be observed in correlation with malfunctioning brain chemistry, but it is also informed by psychological, emotional, and social factors. To reduce addiction as a phenomenon to its purely neurobiological elements is to focus on only one element of a much broader picture: the social, cultural, and environmental factors that influence – and can ultimately help explain just as well – addictive behaviour.

To name but one factor: socioeconomic status can consistently predict a higher prevalence of substance use disorders among lower strata. This does not mean that there is something inherently different in the brain chemistry of people from lower socioeconomic status. It's a result from a combination of correlated factors: higher likelihood of experiencing stress, trauma, and access to areas where substance abuse is more common. Neuroreductionism can explain how a specific brain mechanism leads from stress to drug use, but it cannot explain why that brain would be stressed in the first place, a crucial step in explaining addictive behaviour prevalence among a population.

This is without even mentioning cultural norms and values, which also play a large role in how people approach substance abuse and addiction. Some cultures can have vastly different religious or social rituals, which will shape drinking habits and therefore lead to different levels of alcohol abuse among a population. Once again, a neuroreductionist approach can show us how substances affect the brain, but it doesn't explain why people use them in the first place or why they're more or less likely to lead to addiction depending on the cultural context.

The limitations of neuroreductionism are perhaps most evident in the realm of treatment. If we view addiction solely as a brain disease, the logical conclusion is that the most effective treatments will target the brain. This has led to the development of a range of pharmacological interventions aimed at altering brain chemistry in order to reduce cravings, prevent relapse, or mitigate withdrawal symptoms. While these treatments can be effective for some individuals, they are not universally effective. Many people with addiction find that pharmacological treatments are insufficient on their own and that they require additional support in the form of therapy, counselling, or social services to achieve and maintain recovery.

Additionally, by focusing exclusively on the brain, neuroreductionism can inadvertently reinforce the stigma it seeks to eliminate. The brain disease model was originally developed, in part, to combat the moralistic and stigmatizing view of addiction as a condition resulting from poor decisions or weak character. By emphasizing the underlying biological mechanisms of addiction, proponents of the BDMA hoped to change public perception and encourage the idea of addiction as a medical problem deserving treatment rather than punishment. However, by reducing addiction to a matter of brain chemistry, neuroreductionism can also lead to a rather deterministic view of addicted people as passive victims of their biology, lacking agency or the capacity for change. This narrative could suggest that recovery depends solely on medical or pharmacological intervention, rather than a holistic approach that also considers the psychological, social, and environmental dimensions of addiction.

This danger of an oversimplification in the form of neuroreductionism is particularly evident in the realm of public policy. Policymakers, eager for solutions to the complex issue of addiction, may lean towards neuroreductionist explanations that promise a quick fix to a very complicated problem. For instance, the idea that addiction can be cured with a pill or by targeting specific neural circuits can be very appealing to those in search of cost-effective and easily implementable solutions, as has been the case in US congressional hearings with NIDA (National Institute on Drug Abuse). This can lead to policies that prioritize pharmacological treatments or brain-based interventions at the expense of more comprehensive strategies that consider the full spectrum of factors contributing to addiction.

And this narrow focus can have adverse consequences. Policies that are based primarily on neuroreductionist principles may fail to address the underlying social and environmental conditions that contribute to addiction. Providing treatment options based solely on medication for opioid addictions, for example, can be insufficient on its own, even if it is an important component of a comprehensive treatment strategy. Without addressing issues such as housing instability, unemployment, and access to mental health services, medication alone is unlikely to lead to sustained recovery for many individuals. In this sense, a neuroreductionist approach to policy can result in interventions that are ultimately ineffective in the long term, as they fail to address the root causes of addiction.

Avoiding easy answers from neuroreductionism requires a commitment to a more integrative approach, one that recognizes the interplay between biological, psychological, and social factors in the manifestation of addiction. It is out of this need that arises a "biopsychosocial" model. It calls for a rejection of reductionist thinking in favour of a more nuanced understanding of addiction as a dynamic process that cannot be fully explained by neurobiology alone. This means moving beyond the brain to consider the person as a whole, including their life experiences, their social environment, and their cultural context.

In practical terms, advocating for policies that are informed by this biopsychosocial model of addiction takes into account the complex and interrelated factors that contribute to addictive behaviours. The biopsychosocial model recognizes that while neurobiological factors play a role in addiction, they are only one piece of the puzzle. Psychological factors, such as personality traits, coping mechanisms, and mental health conditions, also play a critical role in the development and persistence of addiction. Social factors, such as family dynamics, peer influences, and community support, are equally important in shaping an individual's risk for addiction and their chances of recovery.

Supporting research that explores the social determinants of health, such as poverty, trauma, and social isolation, is essential alongside studies that investigate the neurobiological mechanisms of addiction. Developing a more comprehensive understanding of addiction that is better equipped to inform effective treatment and policy interventions requires that we broaden the scope of factors that we take into account. This might involve investing in social services that address the root causes of addiction, such as programs that provide stable housing, employment support, and access to mental health care. It might also involve fostering community-based approaches to addiction treatment that emphasize peer support and social reintegration.

This must go hand-in-hand with a public information effort as well. Stigma and the public discourse around addiction is equally affected by neuroreductionims, especially in recent years. While it is important to bring more and more attention to the neurobiological aspects of addiction, they should not overshadow the broader societal issues that influence the development of addiction. This includes addressing the ways in which social inequality, discrimination, and marginalization contribute to the disproportionate burden of addiction on certain populations. Challenging the stigma associated with addiction is equally important, and it can be done by promoting a more holistic and compassionate understanding of the disease, one that recognizes the full humanity of those who struggle with addiction and the complex set of factors that shape their experiences.

Ultimately, the goal is not to downplay neurobiological research in understanding addiction but rather to ensure that it fits into a broader framework that recognizes the full complexity of the disease. In resisting the temptation to reduce addiction to a purely biological phenomenon, we can develop more effective and more ethical treatment and policy approaches, ensuring that those struggling with addiction are supported in a way that meets all of their needs.

So while the knowledge gained from neurobiological research is invaluable, it must be integrated into a more comprehensive understanding of addiction that includes psychological, social, and environmental factors. Only by avoiding the easy answers offered by neuroreductionism can we hope to develop the kind of multidimensional and nuanced approaches to addiction that are necessary to address the challenges posed by this complex phenomenon. This approach promises not only to be more effective in addressing the root causes of addiction but also more ethical, because it respects the dignity and agency of people struggling with addiction and recognizes the full range of their experiences.

On Building Effective and Ethical Policy Constructs

In recapitulating the historical narrative of legislative events that have shaped the course of UK drug policy for that past two centuries, I have shown how the *problematization* of addiction, and the conception of it as a social harm that requires regulation, is more pertinent to the understanding of how drug policy has been shaped than the actual history of addiction itself. By situating "harm reduction" strategies within the context of that legislative event narrative, I've attempted to show the shifting focus of policies towards the consequences and effects of illicit drug use, rather than the substances themselves. In doing so, I've tried to provide some notes on the theory motivating harm reduction policies and their pertinence to the measure of "effectiveness" in discussing drug policy constructs.

I've contrasted two distinct examples of policy constructs that illustrate my thesis on the direction of policymaking (L-E and E-L) and argued for the different levels of effectiveness that each has attained, postulating that said differences in effectiveness are directly tied to their adoption of a medical perspective on the issue of addiction, and more specifically the NIDA brain disease paradigm.

The examples I have mentioned in this book are by no means exhaustive, nor do they pretend to encompass the full picture of UK drug policy constructs and the different dynamics at play in influencing and determining their origin. I've chosen to focus on "harm reduction" strategies for I believe they fit into the narrative of legislative events that have shaped the evolution of the different conceptions of the problem of addiction in liberal governance.

From a conceptual standpoint, we must rethink what addiction means in terms of individual agency. It is indeed not a settled and unanimous notion to consider addiction as a "chronic relapsing brain disease" within the entire field of addiction studies. This neuro-normative label can even be a source of some dissatisfaction among philosophers and scientists hoping for a more realistic and holistic account of this very complex human behavioural phenomenon. A third view, neither neuroreductionist nor "free choice", can exist in our understanding of addiction, one that mixes an interdisciplinary approach from the biopsychosocial realm and provides a unifying model of addiction.

This in turn would help in the movement towards a "depathologization" of addiction, i.e. an understanding of addiction as an inherent aspect of life in a post-industrial society, as made evident in Seddon's book, and thus a progressive move forward for legalization of the practice of psychoactive substance consumption in the abstract, as opposed to the piecemeal argumentation over each and every substance, dissecting and weighing the chemical properties to know which are safe to consume and thus can be permitted. Shifting the object of the argument to the practice of psychoactive substance consumption as an inherent offshoot of the human right of bodily autonomy, instead of the paternalistic model of the State regulating which substance can and ought to be made available to the public.

This book has been an attempt to conciliate the different conceptualizations of addiction, and more specifically argue that a critical assessment of how we understand addiction is necessary in order to construct effective and ethical policy constructs to treat addicted persons, avoiding both a neuroreductionist paternalistic view, while also avoiding a moralizing rationalist view. I have argued that conceptualizing addiction with the view of it as a medical condition is the appropriate course for public health goals of harm reduction. In order to construct an effective and ethical set of policy practices, a neurobiological level of analysis informed by an understanding of the behavioural manifestations of the disrupted neurocircuitry is the most appropriate course.

A contemporary view of addiction from a medicalized conceptual standpoint does not deny the influence of social, environmental, and developmental processes, but instead argues that the brain is the underlying substrate upon which those factors will act. It is therefore ethically paramount that the neuroscientific modelization be properly incorporated into a biopsychosocial framework for understanding addiction, and furthermore that it be at the core of the ethos guiding policy constructs. Understanding the neurobiological pathophysiology is critical for the aetiology of addiction as a disorder, for the development of sound healthcare options, and for the ethical treatment of addicted persons.

What the Future of Addiction Research Should Look Like

Finally, I would like to finish this book by looking to the future and what it might hold for addiction research, how it might continue to shape our ever-evolving conceptualization of this complex phenomenon, and what solutions might be brought about to deal with its many problematic aspects for the individual and society.

Beyond the BDMA

As I hope to have showcased in Chapter 3, it is true that the field of neuroscience has significantly advanced our understanding of addiction, and I would argue that the BDMA has been instrumental in reducing the stigma around addiction by framing it as a medical issue rather than a moral failing. However, the BDMA has not been without controversy, primarily because it tends to oversimplify addiction and reduce it to its neurobiological processes, potentially neglecting the complex interplay of psychological, social, and environmental factors that ought to be integral in a "biopsychosocial" model of addiction.

Future neuroscience research should aim to integrate these factors into a more holistic model of addiction. One promising direction is the exploration of the neurobiological mechanisms underlying resilience and recovery from addiction. While much research has focused on the brain changes associated with addiction, less is known about the brain processes that contribute to recovery. Understanding these mechanisms could lead to the development of new therapeutic strategies that enhance an individual's capacity to recover from addiction.

Additionally, there is a growing interest in the role of neuroplasticity in addiction. Neuroplasticity refers to the brain's ability to reorganize itself by forming new neural connections throughout life. Research in this area could help identify how certain experiences or interventions, such as mindfulness-based therapies or cognitive-behavioural approaches, may promote positive brain changes that counteract the effects of addiction.

Rethinking Agency and Responsibility

As Chapter 2 explored, many philosophical inquiries into addiction have traditionally centred around questions of agency, autonomy, and moral responsibility. The application of addiction to the free will debate, for example, hinges on whether individuals suffering from addiction have diminished control over their actions and, consequently, reduced moral responsibility. The different philosophical perspectives on that debate can lead to varying conclusions about the nature of addiction and the extent to which individuals can be held accountable for their addictive behaviours.

One area in philosophy that might gain traction in the near future is the ethical implications of emerging neurotechnologies in addiction treatment. As neuroscience continues to evolve, technologies such as deep-brain stimulation (DBS) are being investigated as potential treatments for addiction. These interventions raise important ethical questions about consent, autonomy, and the potential for coercion. For instance, if a person with addiction agrees to undergo DBS to reduce their addictive cravings, to what extent is their decision autonomous?

Another philosophical avenue worth exploring is the concept of "moral enhancement" in the context of addiction. Moral enhancement refers to the use of biomedical interventions to improve moral behaviour. In the case of addiction, this might involve using pharmacological agents to reduce impulsivity or once again decrease cravings. Such interventions could also blur the line between treatment and moral manipulation, raising concerns about the potential for abuse or unintended consequences.

Addressing the Social Determinants of Addiction

As this book has amply demonstrated in its final chapters, policy research on addiction has more recently focused on harm reduction strategies. While these interventions have proven effective in reducing the harms associated with drug use, it is important to highlight the need for policies that address the root causes of addiction, such as poverty, social isolation, and even childhood trauma.

Future policy research ought to prioritize the social determinants of addiction, exploring how structural factors like socioeconomic inequality, housing instability, and lack of access to healthcare contribute to the development and pervasiveness of addiction. This approach aligns with the ever-growing recognition that addiction is not merely a personal failing but a complex social issue that requires a comprehensive, biopsychosocial solution.

One promising direction is the development of policies that integrate addiction treatment with other social services. For example, housing programs, which provide stable housing to individuals with addiction without requiring them to achieve sobriety first, have shown promise in improving both housing stability and substance abuse outcomes.

Additionally, there is a need for more research on the long-term impacts of drug decriminalization and legalization policies, some of which were mentioned in this book. While some countries have moved towards more lenient drug policies, the broader societal implications of these changes are still not well understood. Comparative studies that examine the outcomes of different policy approaches across countries could provide valuable insights into the most effective ways to achieve public health goals in the realm of addiction rates.

Shaping Public Perception of Addiction

The way addiction is understood and addressed by society is deeply influenced by the wide variety of disciplinary perspectives talked about in this book: neuroscience, philosophy, and policy. As these fields evolve, they have the potential to reshape public discourse on addiction, moving away from stigmatizing views and towards more compassionate and evidence-based approaches.

Neuroscience has already contributed to a more nuanced understanding of addiction by revealing the brain changes associated with substance use disorders. However, as research continues to uncover the complexity of addiction, it is crucial that public messaging reflects this complexity. Simplistic narratives that portray addiction solely as a brain disease may inadvertently perpetuate stigma by implying that individuals with addiction are irreparably damaged. It is important to promote a more balanced view that acknowledges both the neurobiological and psychosocial dimensions of addiction.

Philosophy also has a role to play in challenging societal assumptions about addiction. By questioning the traditional notions of agency and responsibility, philosophical research can encourage more thoughtful discussions about the moral and ethical dimensions of addiction. This can lead to a shift in how society views addicted persons, from seeing them as morally flawed to recognizing them as individuals grappling with a disease stemming from a complex interplay of neurobiological, psychological, and social factors.

Policy research can also directly influence public health strategies and societal views on addiction. Policies that prioritize harm reduction and address the social determinants of addiction can help reduce the stigma associated with drug use and promote a more compassionate approach to addiction treatment. Additionally, research that highlights the success of biopsychosocial approaches to addiction treatment could lead to a broader adoption of such models, ultimately improving the lives of addicted persons and reducing the costs associated with substance abuse disorders in society.

Overall, and without wanting to state the obvious, the future of addiction research lies in a multidisciplinary approach. One that integrates insights from neuroscience, philosophy, and policy, and which explores areas such as the neurobiology of recovery, the ethics of neurotechnologies, and the social determinants of addiction. In doing so, we can develop a more comprehensive understanding of addiction and inform public health strategies that are both effective and ethical towards addicted persons.

Index

Kolibri 360 GmbH
Ferdinand-Jühlke-Straße 7
99095 Erfurt, Deutschland
produktsicherheit@kolibri360.de